FRIENDS
OF ACPL

ASTRONOMY

Through special arrangement with
Whitman Publishing Company—Racine, Wisconsin

WHITMAN JUVENILES

are now available to schools and libraries in

GOLDENCRAFT BINDING

from

GOLDEN PRESS, INC.

Educational Division

1 West 39th Street—New York 18, N. Y.

19 h 27
19 hours 27 minutes

20 h 27
20 hours 27 minutes

21 h 27
21 hours 27 minutes

22 h 27
22 hours 27 minutes

23 h 27
23 hours 27 m

0 h 27
ur 27 minutes

1 h 27
I hour 27 minutes

2 h 27
2 hours 27 minutes

3 h 27
3 hours 27 minutes

4 h 27
4 hours 27 minutes

The endsheets: **The angle of the Earth's rotation is such that the sun doesn't set on the North Pole for 189 days of each year. These drawings show the position of the sun on such a day, in the far north of Norway.**

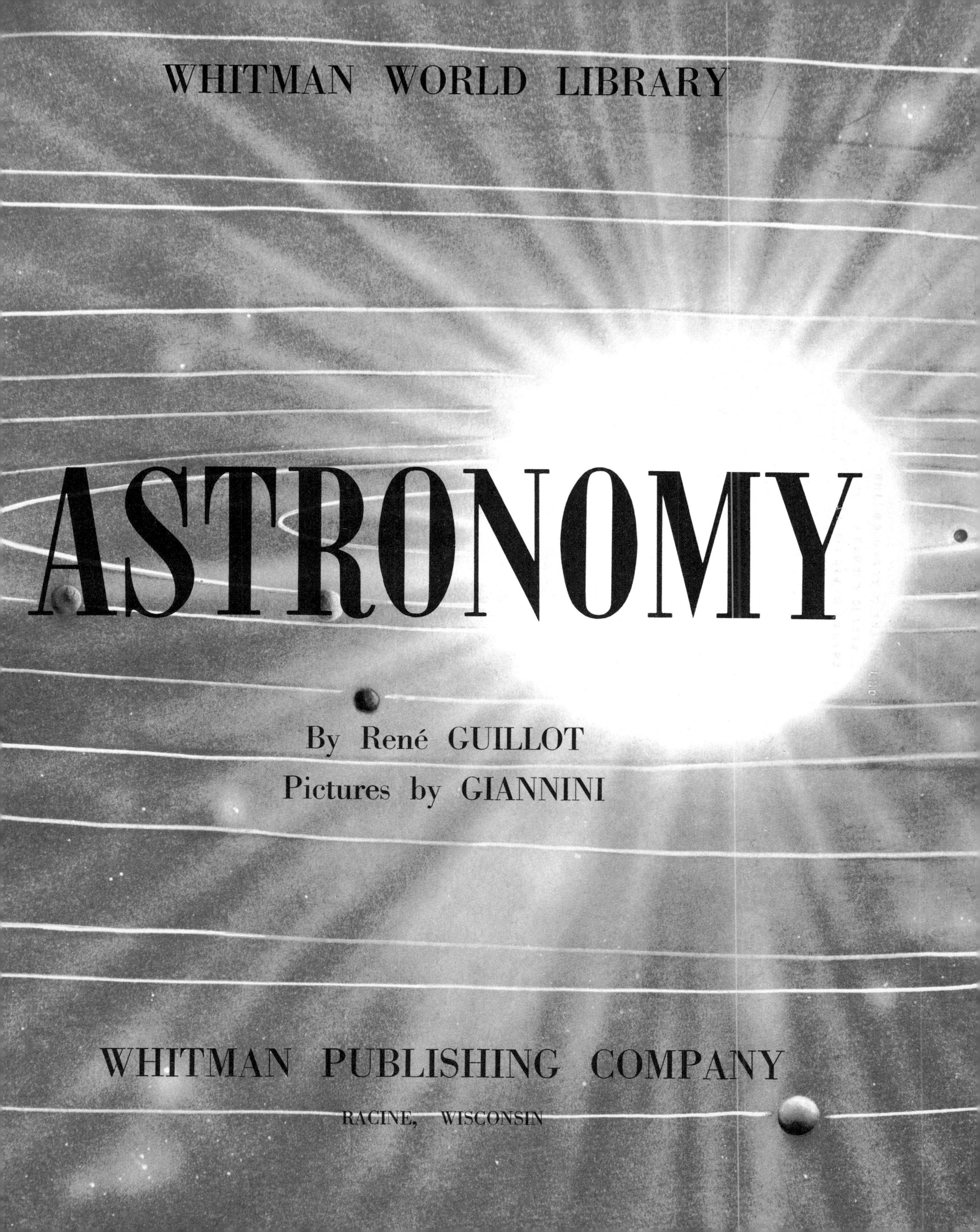

WHITMAN WORLD LIBRARY

ASTRONOMY

By René GUILLOT

Pictures by GIANNINI

WHITMAN PUBLISHING COMPANY

RACINE, WISCONSIN

Library of Congress Catalog Card Number: 63-14672

CONTENTS

THE STUDY OF SPACE

ASTRONOMY is the oldest science, and now, suddenly, it is the most modern, too. Since the earliest times men have studied the skies, fascinated by the sun and the moon, the planets and the stars, wondering what place the earth held in this gigantic universe.

Thousands of years ago, the Chaldeans and the Egyptians made records of the movements of stars and so began astronomy. They realized that the stars changed as the seasons changed and they invented calendars based on the changing heavens. A little later, the ancient Greeks grouped stars together in constellations and named them after animals or mythological heroes. Thus, if we use our imagination, we can see Hercules with his club or the hunter Orion followed by his faithful dog Sirius. Farther to the north we can also make out the Big and Little Dippers which are still known in Latin as the Greater and Lesser Bears. The star on the tip of the Lesser Bear's tail is the Pole Star which the first sailors used to navigate at night. The Romans gave us the names for the planets— Mercury, Mars and Venus.

All through antiquity, and up until only a few hundred years ago, men thought that Earth was the center of the universe and that the sun and the moon and all the stars moved around Earth. They also believed that the stars and planets influenced events on Earth, and so convinced were they of this that many ancient kings kept court astronomers to predict future events and tell them when the positions of the stars were most favorable for making important decisions. Though some of their conclusions may seem unscientific or even ridiculous to us today, their calculations were the basis of all astronomy and their knowledge is still useful to us.

Ptolemy, a Greek living in Alexandria, made a model of the sky which was accepted as fact for over a thousand years. He conceived the universe as a series of domes to which the stars and planets were attached and outside of which were immense gears which made the domes move in different directions. It was not until 1530 that Nicolaus Copernicus published his theory of the solar system and proved that Earth and the other planets revolved around the sun.

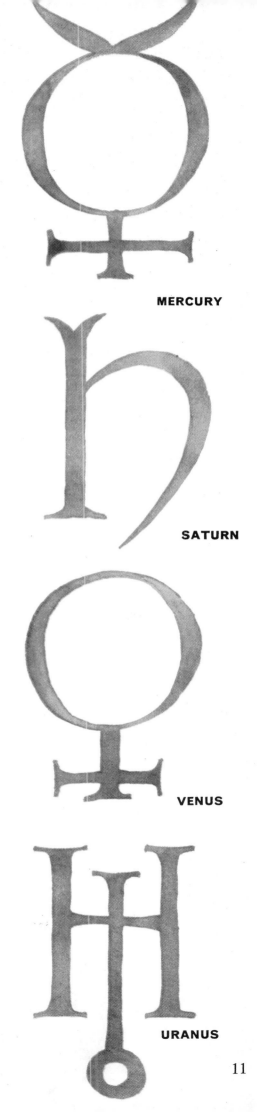

MERCURY

SATURN

VENUS

URANUS

11

Our solar system is but a tiny spot in the galaxy to which we belong. The arrow indicates our position—about 25,000 light-years from the center of the galaxy.

What do we now know about the universe?

We know first of all that it is so colossal that if we measured it in our terms, that is to say in miles, we would have to say millions of millions of millions until our tongues were twisted and we were thoroughly confused. So astronomers measure distance in light-years, or the distance that light travels in one year of our time. Since light travels about 186,000 miles a second (and light travels faster than anything else), a light-year is almost six trillion miles.

Even with the help of light-years we know the universe is so big that we cannot guess at its limits. When you look at the sky on a clear night you can see about three thousand stars. If you should look through a telescope you would see millions more. There are billions of others, too far away to see or to distinguish from a bright mass. Most of the stars you see even without a telescope are so far away that if you traveled at the speed of light you could not possibly reach them in a lifetime.

Each star is a sun, somewhat like ours. Some are smaller, most are larger. Our sun has nine planets revolving around it, and some of those planets, ours for instance, have moons revolving around them. The sun is very close to us in universal terms: Its light takes only 8 1/2 *minutes* to reach us. The

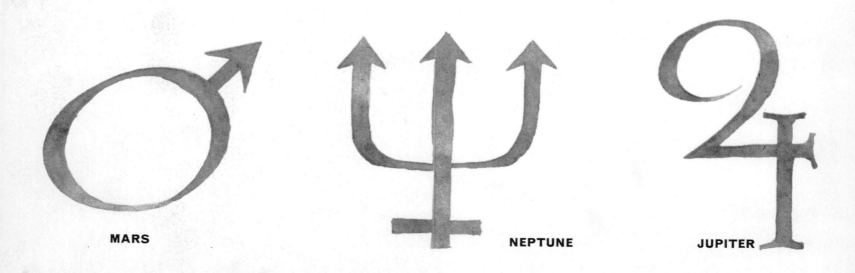

MARS NEPTUNE JUPITER

next nearest star is Alpha-Centauri. Its light takes 4 1/2 *years* to reach us. It is too far away for us to see whether it has planets revolving around it.

Stars are not the smallest "pieces" of the universe. Smaller than these are meteorites, moons, comets, and planets. These are different from stars not only because of their size but because they are made up chiefly of solid matter. They are not hot, hence do not give off light but merely reflect the light of the sun they circle. A group of planets circling around a sun is called a solar system.

Our solar system circles about the center of gravity of our *galaxy* which is a huge discus-shaped conglomeration of stars. The galaxy revolves around its own center of gravity. Our sun, which lies about 25,000 light-years from the center, requires 220 million years traveling at 125 miles per second to make one revolution. This time is known as a cosmic year. Seen from another star, our sun is only a smallish dot near one edge of the galaxy. Earth is not even visible.

But even this galaxy is not enough to fill up space. Whereas once men thought that the universe consisted of the earth with the sun and a few stars circling around it, modern telescopes have made us see thousands of galaxies besides our own, each galaxy made up of millions of sun-stars. Newer inventions, such as radio-telescopes, have allowed us to discover more and more of the universe. And now man's latest achievement, space travel, will let him explore some of the nearest areas of space which until now he has only been able to peer at curiously.

Even as you read this book, newspapers will be publishing new discoveries. Undoubtedly some of these pages will be proved wrong. (For centuries men seemed to have every reason to believe the earth was flat—until it was finally proved round.) Others will seem incomplete. But page by page you will be introduced to a fascinating world whose mysteries are daily being uncovered—the world of space.

PLUTO   **THE EARTH**

The astrologers of the Middle Ages built models of the universe as they knew it. In this old engraving the Earth is still pictured at the center of the universe and the constellations revolve around it.

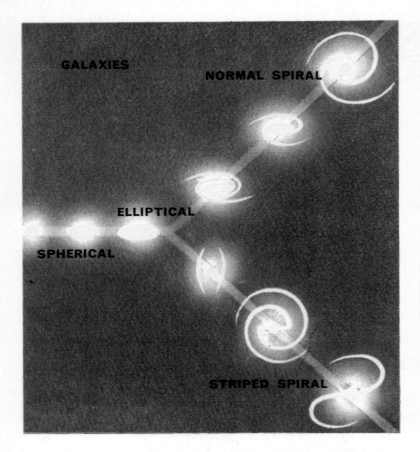

GALAXIES

NORMAL SPIRAL

ELLIPTICAL

SPHERICAL

STRIPED SPIRAL

Perhaps our world began by a series of galaxies which were first elliptical or spherical. They then became either spiral galaxies or galaxies with two arms.

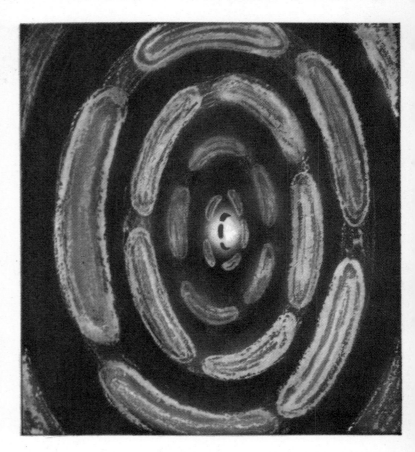

A solar system is born. According to the most recent theory, the skies were filled with whirling clouds of gases. Gradually these clouds condensed, leaving smaller clouds still whirling around them. These clouds in turn condensed, forming the planets.

Right: A map of the world drawn by Andrea Bianco in the year 1439 shows the world flat, surrounded by oceans at the edges of which reigned wild monsters.

THE BEGINNING OF MATTER

MATHEMATICIANS with their numbers and formulas, astronomers, philosophers, and even poets have worked at the immense mystery of the origin of the world. Scholars continue to argue about the problem. There are now two main theories about the beginning of matter, each fascinating partly through the fact that it contradicts the other.

The first one is an astrophysical theory (astrophysics is the branch of astronomy that deals with the physical and chemical characteristics of heavenly bodies) and is the theory of the *static universe*. According to this theory the universe always existed and was always made up of the same mass and energy.

The second theory is founded on astronomical observation. According to it, there was a time, billions of years ago, when nothing existed except for a gigantic mass of hydrogen atoms concentrated in a relatively small space. Hydrogen atoms produce heat when they form larger atoms. The first step in the creation of the world was the explosion of this mass.

The explosion may have lasted only thirty minutes, but during this short time all the "natural" elements were formed such as oxygen, hydrogen, iron, sulphur, calcium, phosphorus, and so forth.

According to this same theory, the second stage of the creation of the world lasted some thirty million years. During this period the universe was an immense and continually expanding sphere of gas.

The third phase was the condensing of the expanding sphere of gas into galaxies of stars and planets. Each of the galaxies or small universes contained millions and millions of suns, but each would split in two, like a colossal amoeba. The splitting up of galaxies continued until the universe became what it is today. It is probably at the end of this third phase that simple bodies combined to form composite bodies which in turn mixed together. Thus planets were born, first whirling spheres of gas, then of liquid, and finally of solid matter revolving around a sun.

Since observations of the sky lead scientists to believe that stars are continually changing their position, perhaps we are still in the third stage of this creation and rushing farther onward from the center of the explosion, wherever it occurred.

UNIVERSAL GRAVITATION

 EARLY scientists were immensely curious about the shape of the earth and anxious to learn its limits. Wise men and priests, thinkers and rulers, all put their heads together. They decided that the earth was flat and surrounded by nothingness and that it stood still in the very center of the universe. But if the earth stood still, how was it supported? The early Greeks decided that the giant Atlas held the earth on his shoulders. The Chinese thought it was carried on the backs of four elephants. The Hindus and the Japanese were convinced it rested on the back of a sacred dragon and a snake.

Thus, in many different places and in many different periods, men believed the earth to be flat as a pan-cake. Limited by this belief, sailors didn't venture far from shore; they were haunted by the fear of dropping over the edge of the world. But later it was sailors who, striking farther and farther into the deep, crossed the oceans and thereby proved that the earth was round.

Photographs of the earth have been taken recently by cameras mounted in rockets. These photographs, taken from a height of two hundred miles, clearly show the curvature of Earth. A space traveler would see the earth as an enormous moon thousands of miles below his rocket. As the rocket zoomed into space, he would see Earth become a smaller and smaller "moon" until it is only a speck of light.

Less than a hundred years later, the simple sight of an apple falling from a tree led the English scholar, Sir Isaac Newton, to seek more explanation of this force and to see how it applied not only to men but to stars. The apple must have fallen straight to the ground, he thought to himself, because it and the earth attracted each other. Since the apple was small and the earth large, the motion of the earth could not be

The Chinese thought the Earth rested on the backs of giant elephants.

The discovery that the earth was round and that men could travel over its entire surface discredited all earlier ideas about the earth being supported from underneath. There was no underside of the world. But if nothing held it up, how were men themselves held to it? Men began to realize that some mysterious force must be attracting them to the earth, and many experiments were performed to discover what kind of force this might be. Some of the most famous experiments were made by Galileo Galilei, an Italian scientist who lived in the late sixteenth century.

The curvature of the Earth is clearly seen in photographs taken from 3,840 miles up by the Thor-Able rocket. Here you can recognize the Mediterranean Sea and a part of Africa and Europe.

seen, and the two came together as the apple moved toward the center of the earth. Newton concluded that the *weight* of the body is in reality the attraction of the earth for the body. This is what is now known as *gravity*. Newton wondered if it was not this mutual attraction of two bodies which caused the moon to orbit around the earth instead of moving in a straight line off into space.

Since Newton's time, scientists working with better equipment and a larger collection of information have been able to prove him right. The gravitational forces extending between the earth and the moon not only cause tides on the earth but also tides on the moon. We usually consider the effect of tides to be limited to the rise and fall of water level in the oceans, lakes, and streams. But the tides also have long-time effects on the motions of both the earth and the moon. From measurements made over a period of many years it has been possible to compute what the relative positions and motions were millions and billions of years ago and what they will become far in the future. Some hundred million years ago the moon was about nine thousand miles from the earth and the earth day was about five hours long instead of twenty-four. A moon month was a little more than five hours. Now, of course, it is about twenty-eight days. Many billions of years in the future the month and day will be equal and will be about fifty-five of our present days. The moon will be much farther away then, since the slower it goes the larger will be the orbit.

Newton's work helped him to confirm the theories of the German scientist, Johannes Kepler, and to put into words the theory of *universal gravitation*. This theory was briefly that:

Two bodies attract each other with a force in direct proportion to the product of their masses. The bigger object will always have more attraction, but the farther the bodies are apart the smaller will be their attraction for each other.

All bodies have this property of gravitation which acts like a magnet and which enables them to attract other bodies.

Even if we jump up we do not fly off. We fall back to the earth, for it attracts us as it did the apple.

Newton's law also explains why the same bodies have different weights at the bottom of the sea than they do on the top of the highest mountain, that is to say, farther or nearer from the earth's center of gravity. When we say a rocket weighs thirty tons, we mean that the gravity of the earth pulls it with a force of thirty tons. When the rocket is launched, and goes into orbit, it requires this thirty tons of pull toward the center of the earth to keep it from going off into space. The force which pulls any

Galileo performed some of his experiments from the leaning Tower of Pisa.

Twirl in your hand a ball at the end of a string. You will feel the centrifugal force tugging the ball from your fingers.

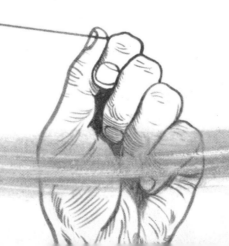

Pioneer IV, launched on March 3, 1959, has become another planet. This small cone, made of gold-plated fiber glass, revolves around the sun in the Asteroid zone, from 88,320,000 to 101,520,000 miles from the sun.

According to Newton's Law of Gravity, all bodies attract each other in direct proportion to the product of their masses, and indirectly in proportion to the square of the distance between them. On the Earth, this attraction is known as weight. A satellite must travel at a speed of approximately 18,000 miles per hour to maintain an orbit of between 350 and 650 miles from the Earth. At this speed, the centrifugal force is equal and opposite to the Earth's gravitational pull.

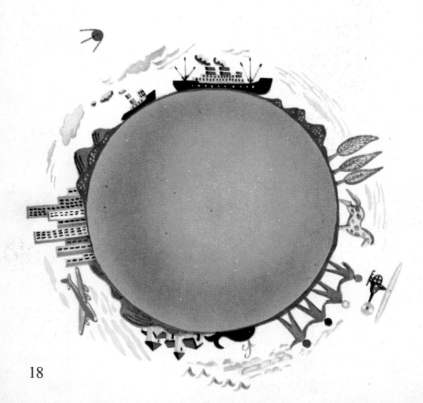

object toward its center of circular motion is called centripetal force. In the case of a thirty-ton rocket in orbit, the centripetal force is thirty tons. Of course, a rocket of thirty tons on the launching pad is likely to become an eight-ton rocket in orbit since this much weight was discarded as burned fuel on the way up. The centripetal force is then eight tons. An object traveling in a curved path so that all the earth's gravitational pull is required to keep its path circular is said to be "weightless." Inside the rocket the space traveler is also weightless. If he is not tied down he can float in his cabin. If he breaks a glass of water the liquid does not spill. By the same token, the broken glass also stays in place around the water and he has to peel it off, like an orange, in order to get at the water, which he then drinks by pricking it with a straw and sucking it out from the inside.

Let us suppose that this spaceship is going toward the moon. As the distance from the earth increases, the gravitational attraction of the earth becomes less. As the moon is approached, its gravitational attraction will increase, and the rocket will reach a point where the earth and moon forces will be equal and opposite. At this point the rocket and its contents will also be in a "weightless" condition. From here on, the moon's attraction will steadily increase until it reaches its full surface value, which is approximately one-sixth as much as at the earth's surface since the moon is so much smaller than the earth.

Although heavenly bodies attract each other mutually, their forces of attraction usually give rise to circular motions around each other or their common center of gravity. (An exception is the special case in which one object is going directly toward another as they approach—as when meteors fall into our atmosphere.) Whirl a stone around on the end of a sling. The force of the stone will almost pull the sling from your hand. This force that pulls the stone away from your hand is called centrifugal force. The force continues to grow stronger as the speed of rotation grows faster.

We can think of the sun as a hand holding an invisible sling at the end of which is the earth. If the sun suddenly ceased to exist, the earth would fly off like a stone released from its sling. At the same time the attraction that draws the earth to the sun would be cut off. Centrifugal force and gravitational force are two opposite forces that balance each other out and that create the equilibrium in our universe.

Today scientists achieve the same sort of equilibrium on a very small scale when they orbit artificial satellites by means of rockets. The American satellite Pioneer V automatically placed itself in orbit when its centrifugal force, caused by its rotation, was exactly balanced by the gravitational force of the sun.

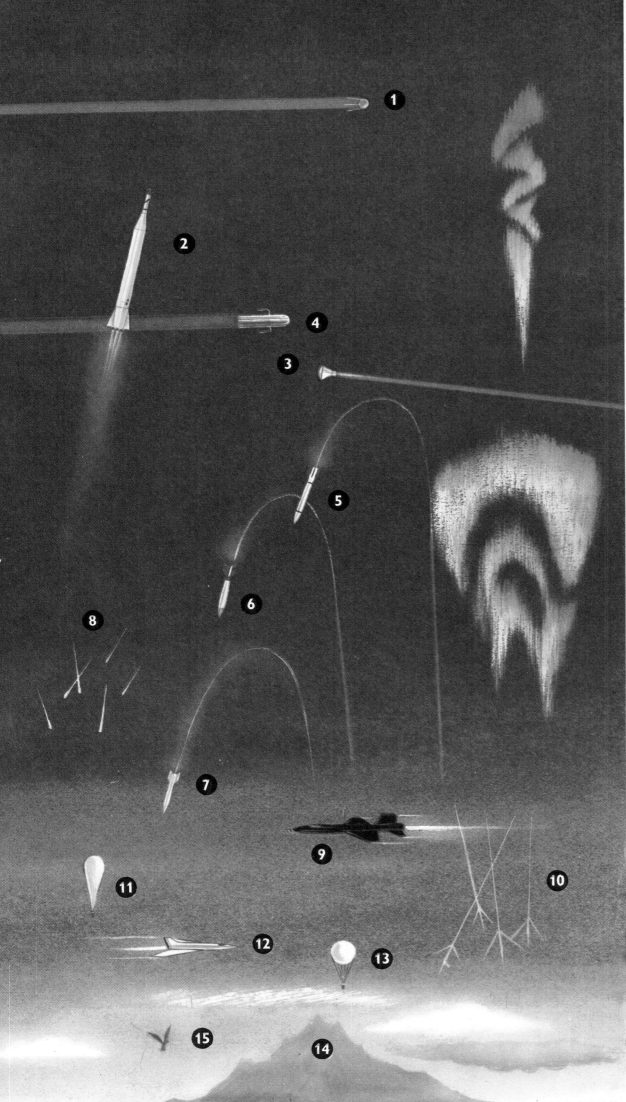

1 Sputnik - 590 miles

2 Atlas rocket - 3,900 miles

3 Mercury capsule - 160 miles

4 Vostok - 138 miles

5 Viking rocket - 130 miles

6 V—2 rocket - 110 miles

7 Wac corporal rocket - 44 miles

8 Meteors - 30 to 70 miles

9 X-15 rocket plane - 57 miles
   (Robert White 1962)

10 Cosmic rays - 6 to 40 miles

11 Sounding balloon - 28 miles

12 Jet fighter - 6 miles

13 Ascension of the "Zenith" - 30,000 feet

14 Everest - 29,141 feet

15 Eagle - 19,685 feet

Near the poles, electrons from the sun are bent by the Earth's magnetism. The light takes on the appearance of a beautiful curtain hung from the upper layers of the atmosphere.

The different levels of the atmosphere are the troposphere, reaching from sea-level to an altitude of 10 miles; the stratosphere, from 10 to almost 60 miles; the ionosphere, from 60 to 500 miles; outer space, which extends from an altitude of 500 miles to the limits of the universe.

A ray of "white" light enters a prism and is decomposed into the seven colors of the rainbow.

THE SKY

WE cannot begin to observe and explore the sky without first studying the phenomena of light and the large layers of atmosphere that surround our earth.

Light

For centuries men have seen the rainbow appear splendidly during a rainfall and have marveled at it. Recently scientists have begun to study light, and as a result they have learned what makes up the rainbow. The bright light that we call daylight appears white to us, but that is only because we cannot see the individual colors when they are mixed. The scientists showed that daylight is composed of electromagnetic rays of the sun which are of seven colors: violet, indigo, blue, green, yellow, orange, and red. This they discovered by breaking up the white rays into their seven components with the aid of a prism. The same view of the *spectrum* can be obtained with a bevel-edged plate of glass, or even by looking through a drop of water. A rainbow appears most clearly during a rainfall in either early morning or evening or when the sun is close to the horizon.

We must look, with our backs turned to the sun, into falling raindrops in order to see a rainbow. The raindrops reflect and refract (bend) the light at slightly different angles for each of the colors. We thus can see separately the different colors in the sunlight. The same sort of thing happens on a much smaller scale at the mouth of a fine-spray hose.

The color of light changes according to the objects the sun's rays meet. In the transparent air the electromagnetic rays meet nothing but tiny dust particles and the light appears white. But light rays traveling through water are first seen as blue, then green, then darker and darker shades as they go deeper through the water.

The first astronauts, after they passed the layer of air covering the earth, found a sky as black as ink. In space there are no dust molecules to catch even the smallest amount of the sun's light.

The layers of the atmosphere

The atmosphere is an envelope of gas which surrounds the globe. All forms of life on Earth—people,

20

Upper layers (1) Lower layers (2) Upper layers (3)

Lower layers (4) Upper layers (5) Lower layers (6)

The winds blow around the Earth in certain cycles which determine the weather. Masses of hot or cold air move over the surface of the globe creating low pressure areas in their wake. New masses of air pour into those low-pressure areas. The air rushing into these areas causes the winds. The dotted line indicates the zone where hot and cold air meet. The main phases of the wind cycle: 1. Masses of hot air rise near the poles (high pressure areas, winds turning clockwise), while masses of cold air descend near the equator (low pressure areas, winds counterclockwise). The region where two currents meet is called the circumpolar storm zone. 2. This sketch illustrates the same phenomenon at sea level, where the trade and anti-trade winds are to be found. 3. Masses of cold air from the upper levels descend near the equator. 4. Cold air currents flow toward the equator. 5. Large circular swirls of mixed hot and cold air masses. 6. At the end of the cycle at sea level hot air masses are at the poles and cold air masses are around the equator. The cycle begins again when hot and cold masses start to mix.

animals and plants—breathe within this envelope which is approximately six hundred miles high. It is made up primarily of a mixture of oxygen, nitrogen, carbon dioxide, and water vapor. The atmosphere becomes thinner and thinner as we climb upward. Every planet has its own atmosphere. But no planet has an atmosphere anything like ours. Except, perhaps, for simple plant structures on Mars, it seems that plant or animal life would be impossible on any of the planets we know.

Scientists have named the first layer of atmosphere the *troposphere*. It extends for ten miles above the earth. The second layer is called the *stratosphere* and stretches about fifty miles above the troposphere. The third and last layer of the atmosphere, the *ionosphere*, stretches about 440 miles above the stratosphere.

The clouds

Clouds exist in the troposphere, which is the layer of atmosphere that contains all weather. They are caused by the continual change of the condition of water vapor in the air, which condenses, then evaporates, or falls as rain. Clouds are masses of tiny drops or crystals of ice which fall very slowly. The passage of air from a hot region to a cold region is sufficient to form a cloud. The slightest air current can make the cloud rise like a balloon and the lightest wind can push it. Fogs are clouds formed by the rapid cooling of air in the lowest layers of the troposphere.

There are four main types of clouds:
—*Stratus clouds* which resemble a gray cloak and stretch very long distances at an altitude of about three thousand feet.
—*Nimbus clouds* which are thick, black clouds, rain carriers, and float at about 3,500 feet.
—*Cumulus clouds*, or fair weather clouds—big, fluffy balls of cotton which float at an altitude of between fifteen hundred and 24,000 feet.
—*Cirrus clouds* which are long, pale ribbons which stretch out at the very top of the troposphere.

The winds

The atmosphere is always moving. Winds move through it much the way that currents move through the water. Major air currents begin at the equator, the hot belt that stretches around the middle of the earth.

Cirrus: 20,000 feet

Cirro-cumulus: 16,000 feet

Alto-cumulus: 13,000 feet

Cumulus: 10,000 feet

Cumulo-nimbus: 2,000 feet

Hot air in the equatorial regions expands, becomes lighter, and rises. The rising of this mass of air creates a low-pressure area in the lowest layer of atmosphere surrounding the equator.

Masses of cold air from the north and south rush into this region of reduced pressure. If the earth stood still, two great winds would always be blowing across the earth's surface, one going from the north toward the equator and one from the south toward the equator. But because the earth moves, the winds are deflected. That is why the *northern trade winds* blow from northeast to southwest and the *southern trade winds* from southeast to northwest.

The *anti-trade winds* of the two hemispheres are, as their name shows, two winds which blow in opposite direction to the trade winds, and above them. They carry warm air from the equator to the North and South Poles. The trade winds and anti-trade winds are winds which never stop blowing.

The *monsoon* is a seasonal wind which blows from the Indian Ocean to the coast of Asia for six months (the summer monsoon) and in the opposite direction

If the Earth were motionless, the trades and anti-trades would blow in the following way: Winds of polar origin would flow toward the equator and those of equatorial origin toward the poles. However, the Earth does spin on its axis at a speed of over a thousand miles an hour, and this speed (well over the speed of sound) deflects the direction of the trade winds to the west. This same speed also causes low-pressure areas to travel from west to east in the direction of the Earth's rotation.

Lower right: **Typhoons—from the Chinese Taiphong or Big Wind—are tropical cyclones originating in low-pressure zones in the Indian and Pacific Oceans (shown in blue on the map). The eye or center of a typhoon (far right, as seen from an airplane) is a small area of calm air about which winds swirl at speeds sometimes reaching 250 miles per hour. This circular eye is apt to be from 3.5 to 5 miles in diameter, while the typhoon itself may be 185 miles wide.** Above right: **This typhoon is seen from the inside. Blue arrows indicate the swirling winds at the edges. The red arrows indicate the center winds which blow upwards.**

Clouds consist of droplets of condensed water vapor held in suspension in the troposphere. The degree of their visibility depends on their state of condensation.

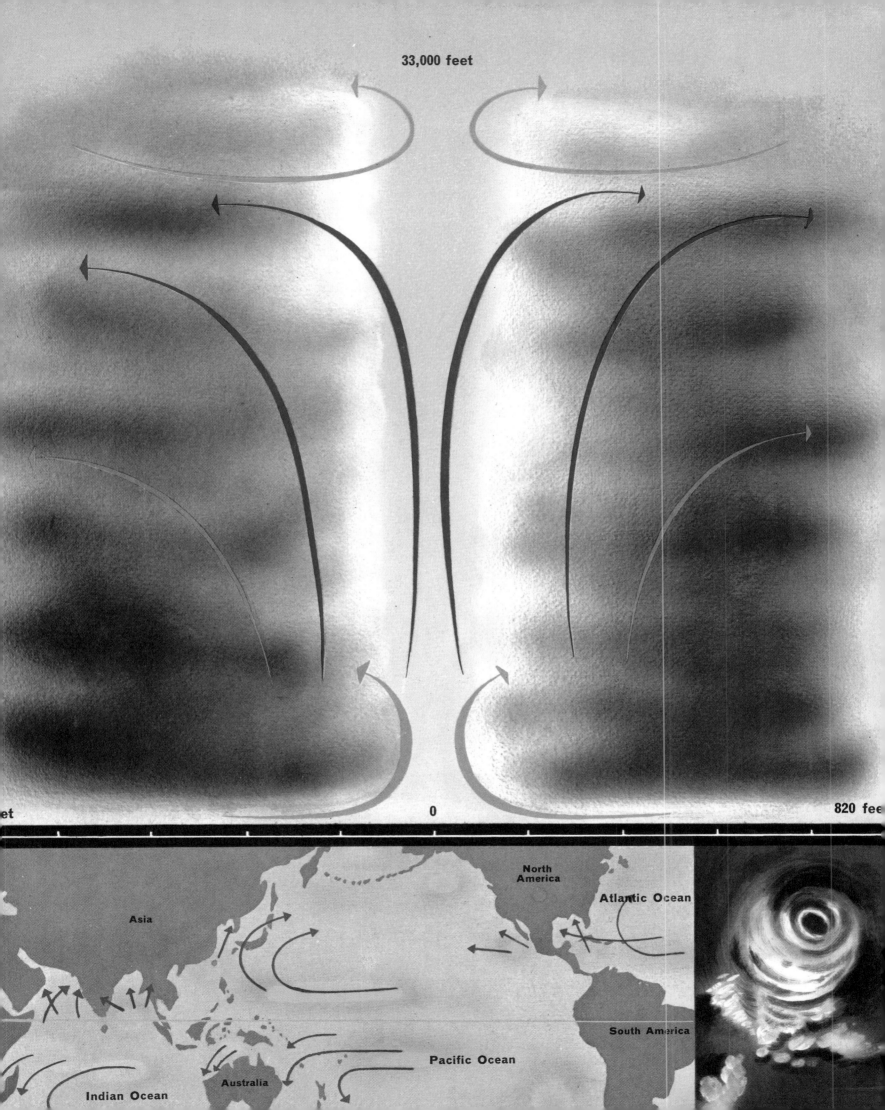

33,000 feet

feet   0   820 feet

Asia

North
America

Atlantic Ocean

Pacific Ocean

South America

Indian Ocean   Australia

According to this fifteenth century engraving, medieval astrologer-astronomers imagined the sky as an immense spherical dome. Behind this so-called "wall of knowledge" lay the mysterious gears which, according to them, made all the stars turn about the Earth.

the following six months (the winter monsoon). During the first six months the land surfaces, warmer than the sea, cause the air to expand. The wind changes direction at the beginning of winter when the earth cools and sends the air currents whistling back.

A tropical *cyclone*, named, according to its geographical position, typhoon, hurricane, or simply cyclone, is a center of very low pressure which forms near the equator and results in a gigantic air movement. This colossal phenomenon is characterized at its center, the cyclone's eye, by a relatively calm atmosphere and an almost clear sky. There are violent, whirling winds outside of the eye, which rush upward. The first converge toward the center, sucking up the surrounding mass, while the second throw air up vertically. Here clouds and rain are abundant.

Hurricanes move somewhat like tops. They are found frequently in waters around China and Japan where they are called typhoons. They are dangerous on the sea and on land, for they tear up everything in their path. They are capable of swallowing up large ships and wiping out all life on coast lines that they hit head-on. (However, if they were seen from high up in space, all the winds in the troposphere turned into hurricanes would still look like a tempest in a small teapot.)

The skies

The first men, who had only their eyes with which to study the moon and the stars, were amazed by and afraid of the secrets of the skies. At night they went to sleep never certain that the sun would rise again the next morning. They must have been very puzzled by the daily cycle of dark and light that takes just twenty-four hours. Ancient scholars, working on these questions later, thought that stars were attached to an enormous, round canopy which turned from east to west.

When we are in a moving train, telephone poles seem to go past us at the same speed at which the train is traveling, while actually we know they are standing still. If we spun like a top at the center of a merry-go-round that was standing still, the wooden horses around us would seem to be moving. The same thing happens with the skies. The earth, spinning us completely around every twenty-four hours, makes the stars appear to be moving. One single star, the polestar, or North Star, seems to be very nearly at the top of the canopy. For centuries sailors have guided themselves by it. But even it is not standing still, and though we now find north by it, men will, in a few thousand years, use other stars which will then lie nearer the earth's axis.

24

The Milky Way is that part of our own galaxy which is visible to the naked eye.

OUR GALAXY - THE MILKY WAY

WHEN we look out our windows on a summer night, a milky band seems to spread like a ribbon across the sky. We call it the Milky Way. What we are seeing is our galaxy, seen through its fullest width at that time of the year. The stars in it are clustered so thickly that, to our eyes, they melt into one whitish mass.

Our galaxy is a gigantic agglomeration of stars and planets whose exact number we will probably never know (around thirty billion!). This enormous galaxy has a radius of fifty thousand light-years and a thickness of fifteen or twenty thousand light-years. The stars in the disk rotate about the center, with those near the outer rim requiring about 300 million years to make one revolution.

The signs of the zodiac

Six thousand years ago, in Chaldea, in the valley of the Euphrates River, astrologers charted and gave names to a dozen special constellations, or groups of stars, in the heavens. These constellations were special because each month the sun rose in turn in one of them. The twelve months of the year were therefore each linked with one of the signs in this celestial family, which is called the zodiac or "ring of animals" since most of the twelve constellations were given the names of animals.

The signs of the zodiac are Aries, Taurus, Gemini, Cancer, Leo, Virgo, Libra, Scorpio, Sagittarius, Capricorn, Aquarius and Pisces.

In ancient times men thought that the stars influenced their lives. They believed their fate was already written in the heavens at their birth, depending upon the month and zodiacal sign under which they were born. This superstition has become firmly embedded. Even today people have their horoscopes read.

The constellations

The Milky Way encircles the globe with its sometimes twinkling, sometimes misty, white haze. We see one part of the sky if we live in the Northern Hemisphere and another part if we live in the Southern Hemisphere. In North America we see the Milky Way spreading around the sign of the Swan. In Argentina, it

Sultans and Caliphs kept astrologers in their courts who already had a vast knowledge of the skies. The zodiac played a major role in their lives. (The Caliph of Bagdad about 1000 A.D.; from a document from the British Museum).

The twelve signs of the zodiac were already well known in Hipparchus' day (second century B.C.).

is seen near the Southern Cross. The equator is the only place in the world where men can see stars and constellations of both hemispheres during the course of the year. Thus, when mapping the heavens, we must map the two hemispheres separately.

Travelers who first sailed around the South Cape saw, as a poet expressed it, "new stars climb above the horizon." They beheld, toward the South Pole, the shining group of the Southern Cross. And, since they had already sailed in the waters of the Orient and Africa, they named the new constellations that they saw after animals that inhabited those sunny lands: the Chinese peacock, the African toucan, and others.

In the Northern Hemisphere the best-known constellation is the Big Dipper, which the Chinese first likened to a stewpan. Its outline consists of four stars, and it has a "handle" of three more stars almost in a straight line.

If we extend by five the length of the handle of the Big Dipper, we come to the polestar, or North Star. This is at the extreme end of the handle of the Little Dipper.

Over the centuries, because of very slow movements of the Milky Way, the polestar has been slightly changing its place. In twelve thousand years we will no longer be able to tell north by it but will use Vega, the brightest star of the Lyre constellation.

The constellations that we see above us in the summer are different from the ones we see in the fall or winter. As the earth spins its yearly orbit around the sun, certain constellations are obscured by the bright light of the sun which comes between us and them. Even at night, when we see no light, they are blotted out of our sky. But at the same time, certain others, which had been blotted out before, become visible. Each season brings us not only a change in the weather, but a change in the sky as well.

If we draw an imaginary line that extends the handle of the Big Dipper we find, in early spring, a magnificent orange-red star. This is Arcturus, in the Drover constellation alongside the Northern Crown.

At this time, in the zodiac, on the opposite side of the sky from the Big Dipper, we see the constellation of the Lion which, rising majestically in the evening, has Regulus as its brightest star.

As summer approaches, the heavens are more filled than ever with stars. The Lyre appears in one arm of the Swan Cross, with Vega, the most brilliant star in the sky at this time of year. A little farther, approximately in the opposite arm of the Swan Cross, we see the three golden points of the Eagle. The central one is Altair.

One of the largest of the known stars is Antares, the bright red star in the middle of Scorpio. In ancient times Scorpio was pictured being chased around the zodiac circle by the Archer (Sagittarius).

In the autumn sky we see the square of Pegasus, which looks like the Big Dipper upside down, with Andromeda at the end of the extended handle. We should not be surprised to find the Chariot, or rather Cassiopeia and Perseus, following behind it. Their names are closely linked in mythology. Perseus, one of the heroes of ancient Greece, was the son of Zeus. He cut off the Medusa's head and its blood gave birth to Pegasus, the winged horse. Astride Pegasus, Perseus flew to the rescue of Andromeda who was threatened by a sea monster, and after saving the goddess he married her.

When winter comes, the charioteer drives his four-horsed chariot in a snow-laden sky. Capella, "The Goat," the fifth star of that constellation, is a giant star. Its diameter is 9,000 to 12,000 million miles. But here again large numbers fail to signify. We shall get a better idea of the dimensions of this star if we say that Capella could hold within it our whole solar system.

During the early hours of our winter nights, we can admire Orion. Four stars in this constellation form the points of a rectangle. At the diagonally opposed points there are two giant stars, Rigel, a white star, and Betelgeuse, a bright red star. These two stars, millions of times brighter than the sun, are more than three hundred light-years away from our earth. Within the rectangle there are three stars in a line, the Three Magi, also known as Orion's belt.

North of Orion, the Pleiades make up a beautiful star mass. To the south we see Sirius, the Dog Star. Though not the largest, it is the most beautiful and the brightest star in the sky. In diameter it is only twice the size of our sun, but it is very close to us compared with the astronomical distance of other stars: about 8.6 light-years. Its brilliance is due to its nearness.

Star masses and nebulae

Constellations are clusters of stars.

A cluster is called "open" when we can see the individual stars in it with the naked eye or with an ordinary telescope. The Pleiades, the Hyades in Taurus, the Coma Berenice, and the Praesepe cluster in Cancer are examples of open clusters.

Other clusters are called "globular" because when we look at them without the aid of a telescope they appear as milky white spots. It takes very powerful telescopes to distinguish the individual stars which form it. Globular clusters are generally much farther away and the distance between the stars in the cluster is a thousand times the diameter of the solar system. Messier 13, in the Hercules constellation,

The celestial North Pole is that spot in the heavens where the north-south axis of the Earth would reach if it were extended. The star nearest this Pole, and the pilot star for all navigators, is known as the polestar or North Star. You will find it shining brightly at the tail of the Little Dipper (Ursa Minor). From calculations made by Chinese astronomers during the reign of the Emperor Hwang-Ti, we know that the star closest to the Pole in 2700 B.C. was what we now call Alpha Draco. By the year 3500 A.D. our present queen of the skies will be replaced by Gamma Cepheus.

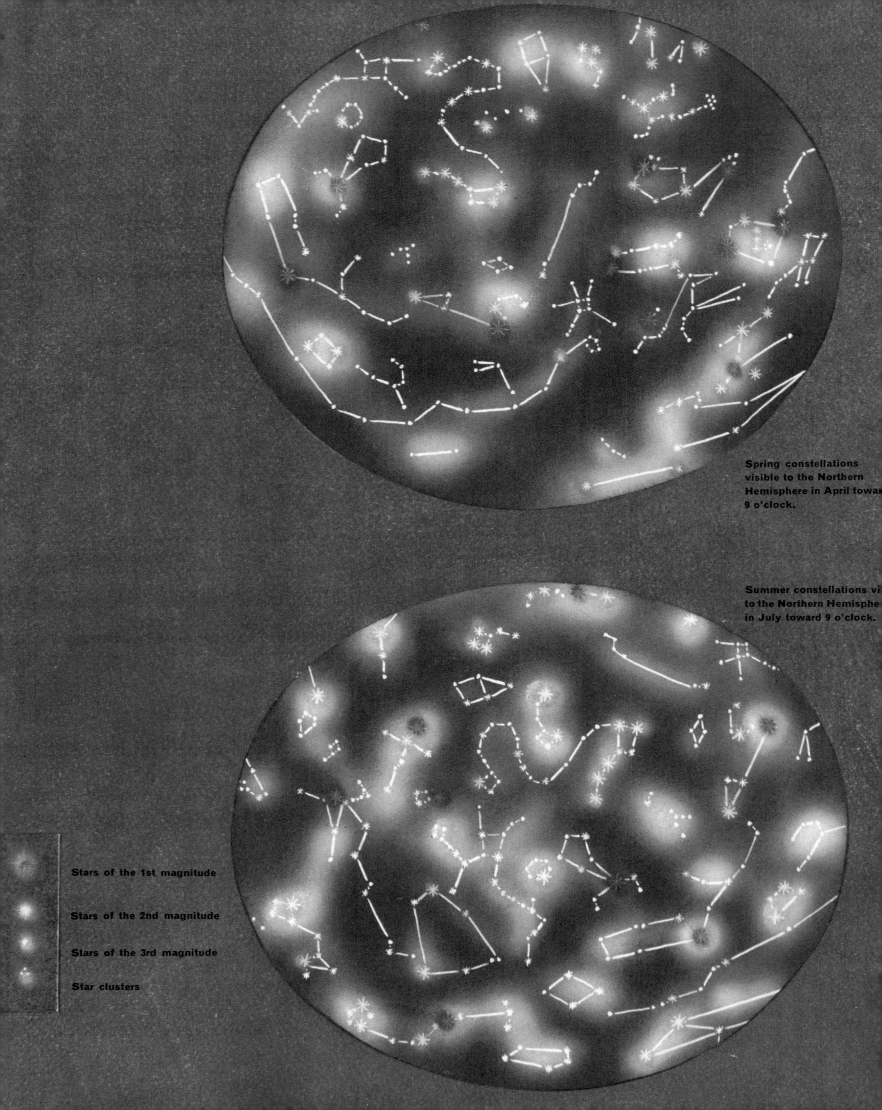

Spring constellations
visible to the Northern
Hemisphere in April towar
9 o'clock.

Summer constellations vi
to the Northern Hemisphe
in July toward 9 o'clock.

Stars of the 1st magnitude

Stars of the 2nd magnitude

Stars of the 3rd magnitude

Star clusters

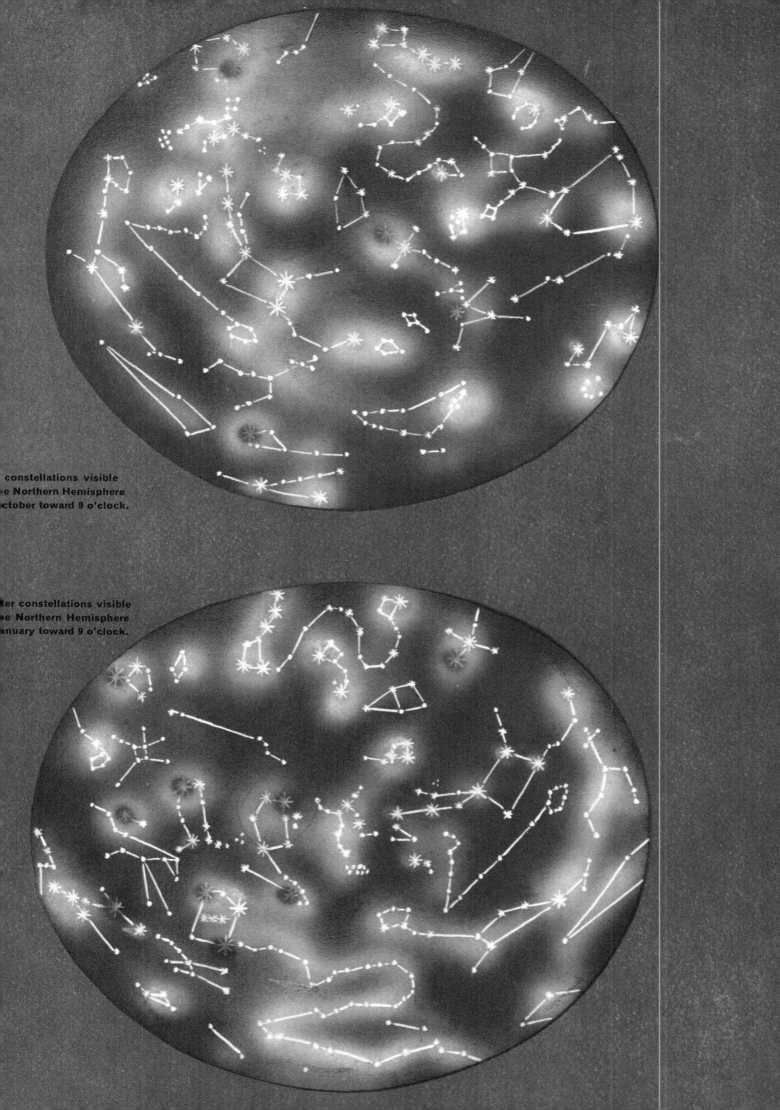

constellations visible
e Northern Hemisphere
ctober toward 9 o'clock.

ter constellations visible
e Northern Hemisphere
anuary toward 9 o'clock.

Different types of nebulae: diffused nebula (the **Crab Nebula**), spiral nebula (nebula in the **Great Bear**), spherical nebula (the **Owl Nebula**).

and the Toucan cluster, which contains almost fifty thousand stars, are seen by us as only two sparkling dots. Through the telescope each of them is a magnificent sight, a blazing ball of stars.

The French astronomer Messier made a catalogue in the eighteenth century in which he listed mysterious spots which looked somewhat like comets but were not. He called them *nebulae*, which in Latin means clouds, and gave them numbers rather than names. As telescopes improved, it turned out that

some of Messier's "clouds" were actually star clusters (that is why the Hercules cluster mistakenly got its name of Messier 13) while others were indeed clouds of gaseous material mixed with dust. Some nebulae have dark spots through which we cannot see. Scientists think these are areas where the gas is more concentrated. Others appear light and fluffy but are actually heavy and huge. The seemingly small nebula around the middle star of Orion's Sword is so big that light takes thirty years to cross it.

Left: **The temperatures of stars increase according to their color, from red to pale blue.**

Right: **The elliptical nebula in Andromeda seems to consist of a densely brilliant nucleus surrounded by two milky arms in the form of a spiral. Two small nebulae, companions of Andromeda, can be seen clearly on the right.**

Stars are shining heavenly bodies made up of very hot gases. Our sun is a star. Its light travels the 93 million miles that separate it from our planet in 8 1/2 minutes.

After the sun, the star nearest to us is the Alpha of the Centaur. It is 26 million million miles away and its light takes 4 1/2 years to reach us. Astronomers have not yet been able to determine whether planets orbit around it.

Certain stars are cooling off or have already cooled off. In some cases their light is only just reaching us although they ceased to give off light thousands of years ago. We may be looking at stars today which were no longer giving light in the year 1000 A.D. when the Vikings were first sighting the shores of North America.

The color of stars varies from dark red for the cold stars, to yellow, to white or to bluish white for the hottest.

Since prehistoric times many stars have undergone vast changes of color and brightness.

Astronomers have observed that these changes of brightness vary considerably according to the star. Some of them change in the course of months or even hours. One of them will suddenly become unusually bright, then fade again to a small speck in the sky. These stars are called *novae*. A nova is a star on which sudden explosions are probably taking place. Sometimes a nova will disappear forever after its brief brightness. Other times it will go back to normal size and perhaps explode again a few months, years, or centuries later.

Gravitation causes some stars to travel together. Some travel in pairs, rotating about their common center of gravity. We see first one, then the other. These are called double stars. They may originally have been one star which split in half. There are also stars which travel in groups of three and four.

Shooting stars which streak across the sky leaving a fiery trail are not stars at all but *meteors*, which are fragments or particles falling into our atmosphere. Such particles are floating in space, and if they come near enough to the earth they are pulled in by gravity. These metallic or stone lumps are usually not much bigger than gravel. Heated by the friction of our atmosphere, they light up and often burn up into gas, which explains why we see them for such a short time (often only seconds). We will say more about meteors when we talk of asteroids in our solar system.

Shooting stars, fireballs, and meteors are the debris of stars which have exploded in a cosmic cataclysm. Showers of shooting stars are most frequent in May, August, and November.

This eighteenth century print shows the famous English astronomer Herschel making a telescope.

BINOCULARS AND TELESCOPES

SINCE ancient times the enlarging properties of lenses have been known. The earliest convex (outward curving) lenses which enlarged objects viewed through them were not made of glass. The Emperor Nero, who could not see beyond the end of his nose, used a large emerald to help him to read and write.

Later, glass spectacles were made.

Sailors have a Dutch optician, Hans Lippershey, who lived at the beginning of the seventeenth century, to thank for the first telescope. It was so constructed as to enlarge the image of distant objects, thus making them appear to be closer to the observer. This telescope, called a spyglass, was a tube with two convex lenses at the ends; the lenses were as thick as those of spectacles used by nearsighted people.

A telescope consists of two main lenses: the *objective* and the *ocular*. The objective is at the far end of the telescope and nearest to the object being observed. It collects the light. Closest to the eye, at the near end of the telescope, is the ocular. The ocular does the magnifying. Lippershey's first telescope had simply two magnifying lenses. Later he constructed one with an objective and an ocular lens. The image it gave, however, was upside down. Although an upside-down image is impractical for looking at things on Earth, for objects far away in the heavens it makes little difference. Today astronomers still use telescopes very much like Lippershey's, contenting themselves with an upside-down image that is nevertheless clear.

At about the same time that Lippershey built his telescope, Galileo was building one for himself. Galileo used a concave (inward curving) instead of a convex lens for the ocular. The concave lens intercepted the light before it came to an upside-down focus. Galileo's telescope thus produced an erect image. For this reason it is still used in "opera glasses." But it is no longer used in astronomy because it will not produce an image on a photographic plate.

For centuries astronomers worked alone. In their makeshift observatories these isolated observers and mathematicians tried, by their calculations, to understand the movements in the universe. The instruments they used they had to make for themselves. Sometimes they spent years at polishing and shaping the lenses that went into their telescopes. They received little encouragement from the world and sometimes were even condemned for their beliefs.

The Yerkes Observatory in America houses the largest astronomical lens in the world (40-inch aperture). The first refractor telescope, invented by Lippershey, was a simple system of two converging lenses in which the eyepiece served to enlarge the tiny image obtained by the lens. As this second image was reversed, today's telescopes include a system of two inverting lenses between the lens and the eyepiece. In Galileo's telescope, the image was not reversed, since the eyepiece was a divergent lens.

A diagram of the principle of an astronomical telescope: Oc = eyepiece; Ob = the lens; i_1 = the image of the distant object produced by Ob; i_2 = the image of i_1 produced by Oc.

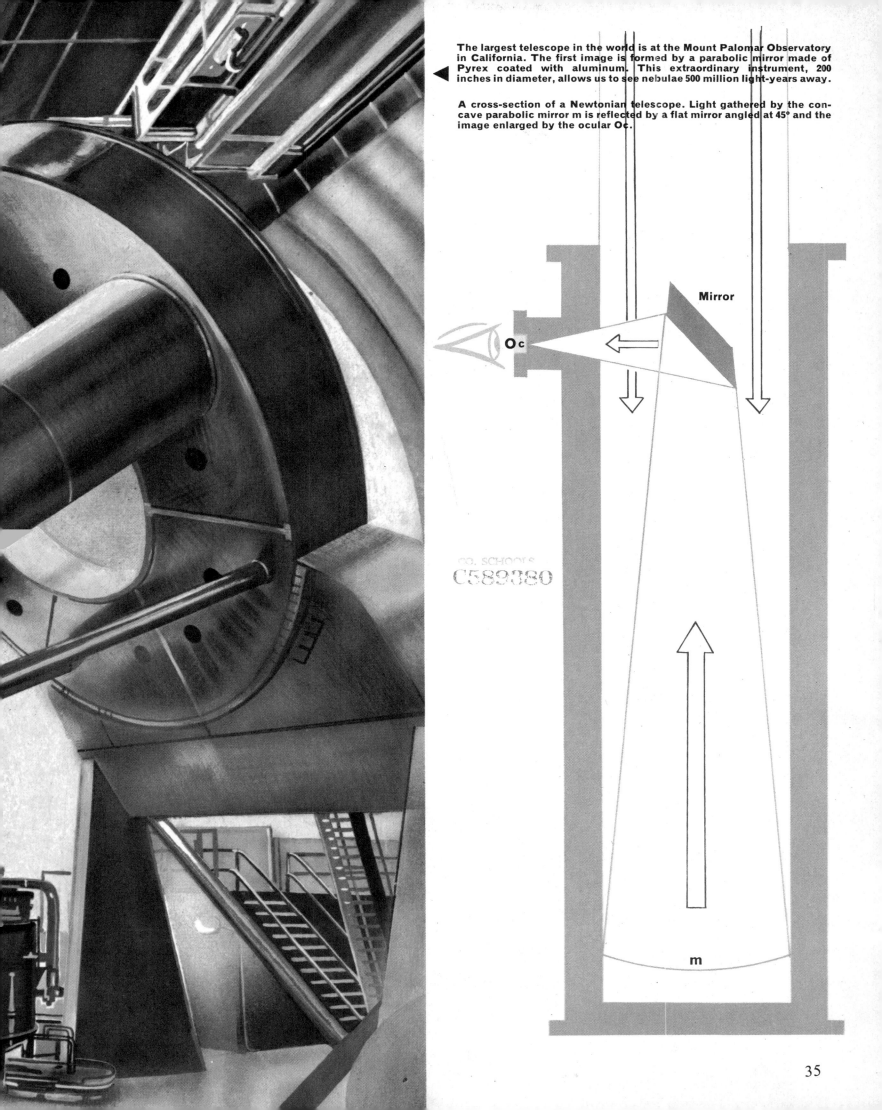

The largest telescope in the world is at the Mount Palomar Observatory in California. The first image is formed by a parabolic mirror made of Pyrex coated with aluminum. This extraordinary instrument, 200 inches in diameter, allows us to see nebulae 500 million light-years away.

A cross-section of a Newtonian telescope. Light gathered by the concave parabolic mirror m is reflected by a flat mirror angled at 45° and the image enlarged by the ocular Oc.

Mirror

Oc

m

From remote antiquity until the end of the Renaissance, comets (particularly Halley's periodic comet) disturbed men. Some observers thought they saw forests of swords and spears, while to others they appeared to be monsters with human faces or streaks of blood. Still others, like the artists responsible for this sixteenth century engraving, saw the armies of Islam about to conquer the skies of Christendom.

The radio telescope at Jodrell Bank is 300 feet high, and its parabolic mirror is 250 feet in diameter, weighing over 2,000 tons. This metal giant is the sharpest hearing device in the world. It can be tilted on a horizontal axis, and the four supporting trucks which swivel it about on a 340-foot circular track move with the precision of finest clockwork. ►

Today's astronomers have at their disposal observatories and equipment that are completely mechanized. Engineers design their instruments and computing machines perform their calculations. Telescopes have taken on gigantic proportions. The moving dome of the Yerkes Observatory has within it the largest refracting telescope in the world. The objective lens has a diameter of forty inches. A base thirty-six feet high contains the complicated mechanism which turns and points the instrument. The observer, when his eye is placed against the ocular, is sixty feet away from the objective lens.

Lippershey's telescope and the Yerkes telescope are refracting telescopes. They catch the light through a lens and then magnify the image. There is another kind of telescope, a reflecting telescope, which works a little differently.

In a reflecting telescope there is no objective lens. The light falls directly into the tube and onto a mirror at the bottom of the tube. The mirror reflects the light upward where another small mirror reflects it to the ocular. The most powerful reflecting telescope in the world is the Hale reflector, at the

Palomar Observatory in California. Its main mirror is two hundred inches wide and weighs 14 1/2 tons. Astronomers using the telescope must take an elevator to reach their observation post in front of the ocular and the smaller mirror. Far bigger reflecting telescopes than refracting ones can be built because supports can be put behind the mirror whereas they cannot be put behind the objective lens. Being larger, reflectors can pick up more light than refractors and show objects at a greater distance.

Telescopes mounted with special apparatus allow us to photograph different parts of the heavens. As the earth turns, the automatic device keeps the objective lens focused on the chosen stars and this allows the photographic plate to be exposed for the great length of time that is needed to photograph such a dim light from so many millions of light-years away. Often we see clearly on a photograph stars we see only dimly through the telescope.

This stick is not broken as it appears but merely thrust under the surface of the water. Light changes direction as it passes from one medium to another. This is known as refraction.

RADIO TELESCOPES

STARS so far out in the infinity of space that they cannot be seen by the most powerful of telescopes can nevertheless be detected by radio.

All stars, even our sun, emit two kinds of rays: light rays and radio-electric rays. The presence of clouds, nebulae, and other bodies will often block light rays, whereas the more penetrating radio-electric waves can find their way through them. Electronic telescopes can pick up these waves and record their frequency and intensity. We can receive radio signals from some stars too distant to be seen by telescope. In this extraordinary unseen world the first constellation to be discovered was the constellation of the Swan in 1946. Six years later it was seen with the aid of the powerful Hale telescope at Mount Palomar.

The largest radio telescope is the one at Jodrell Bank in England. The antenna is in an enormous inverted bowl eighty-two yards in diameter. This bowl is turned toward the portion of the heavens to be "observed," and it picks up the radio-electric waves somewhat like a mirror picks up light rays. All the rays are funneled into the center where, by striking a sensitive surface, they are converted into electric currents and amplified. Sometimes the electric currents activate a needle which graphs the rays on a chart. This makes a more permanent record.

The telescope at the Yerkes Observatory and the Mount Palomar telescope can record stars millions of light-years distant. Radio telescopes reveal the existence of worlds even farther away. They have pushed our knowledge of skies a big step forward.

NEPTUNE

SATURN

THE SOLAR
SYSTEM

WE do not know the number of solar systems in
the universe, but there are certainly many.
Each star is a sun, somewhat like ours, but all
except our sun are too far away for us to see the planets that revolve around them. Our solar system is
therefore the only one that we are familiar with. It
is about 25,000 light-years out from the center of
our galaxy, the Milky Way. The star that is at the
center of our solar system is our sun, and around it
revolve nine planets, their thirty-one moons, and
countless other smaller bodies.

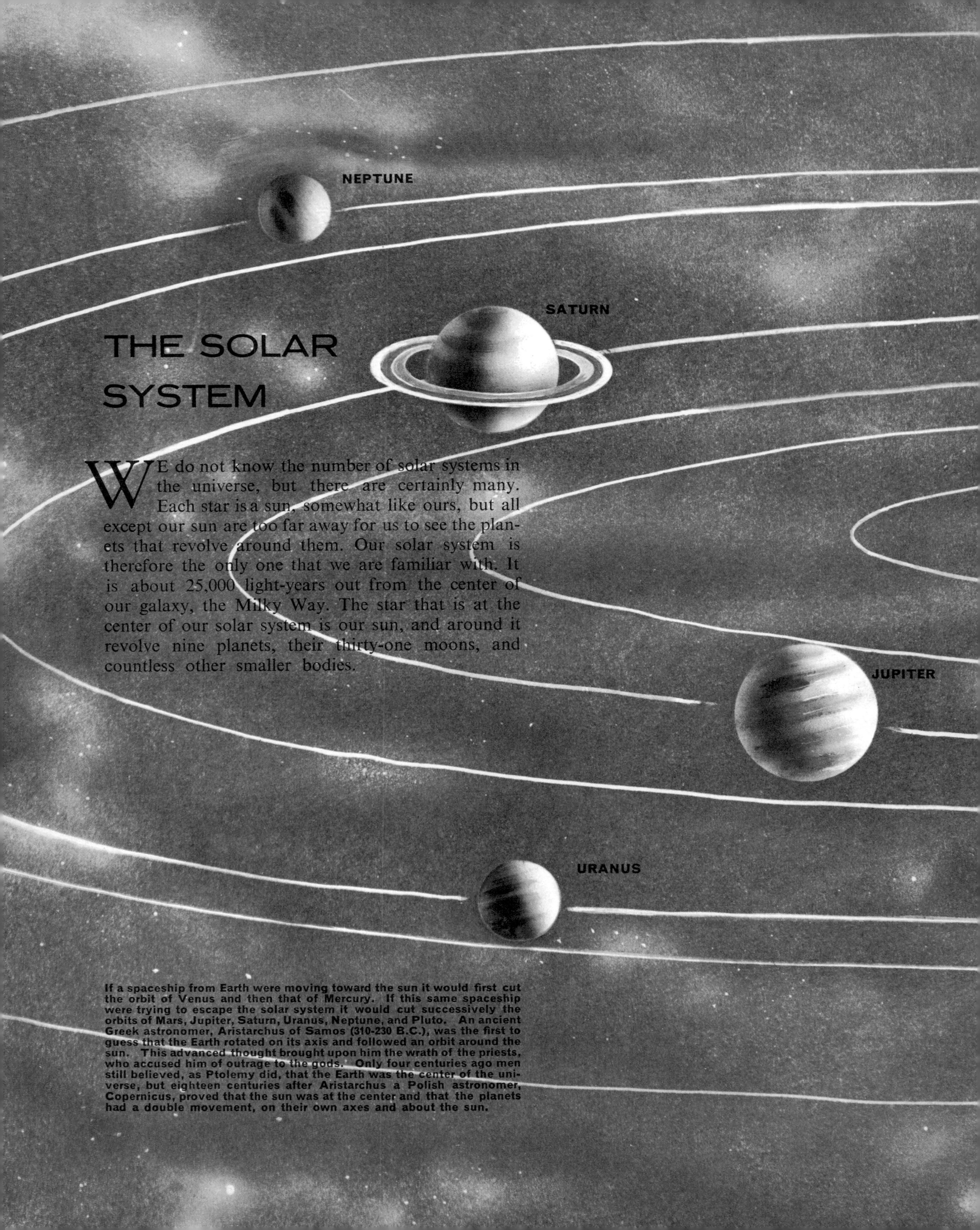

JUPITER

URANUS

If a spaceship from Earth were moving toward the sun it would first cut
the orbit of Venus and then that of Mercury. If this same spaceship
were trying to escape the solar system it would cut successively the
orbits of Mars, Jupiter, Saturn, Uranus, Neptune, and Pluto. An ancient
Greek astronomer, Aristarchus of Samos (310-230 B.C.), was the first to
guess that the Earth rotated on its axis and followed an orbit around the
sun. This advanced thought brought upon him the wrath of the priests,
who accused him of outrage to the gods. Only four centuries ago men
still believed, as Ptolemy did, that the Earth was the center of the universe, but eighteen centuries after Aristarchus a Polish astronomer,
Copernicus, proved that the sun was at the center and that the planets
had a double movement, on their own axes and about the sun.

The planets are more or less round and travel around the sun in an elliptical orbit. An ellipse is the name we give to a slightly flattened circle. The planets are kept in their orbits by the sun's gravitational pull in the same way the moon is kept in its orbit around us.

In the order that they circle around the sun the planets are: Mercury, Venus, Earth, Mars, Jupiter, Saturn, Uranus, Neptune, and Pluto. The word *planet* means a wanderer. Although planets stay on a regular path, they appear to us to wander from constellation to constellation. That is how they first came to astronomers' attention. Actually, only the five nearest to the sun are visible in the sky without the aid of a telescope.

It is interesting to note the sizes of the planets compared with the size of the sun. The largest planet, Jupiter, is one tenth the size of the sun. If the sun were a tennis ball, Jupiter would be a marble; Saturn, a large pea; while Mercury, the smallest, would be the tiny head of a pin. The six others would be varying sizes of pearls. All nine of the planets could easily fit inside the sun.

The closer the planets are to the sun, the shorter the trip they have to make. Mercury goes around the sun four times in the twelve months it takes us to make our round. Pluto, on the outside of the ring, takes almost 250 years to make its orbit. Although not all travel at the same speed, all travel in the same direction.

When we look at the skies on a starry night, Mars, Venus, and Jupiter appear to us to be simply stars. But if we look at them through a telescope we can see that the planets now become discs of light, whereas the stars remain points of light. Also, stars twinkle from changes in our atmospheric density, while the discs of light that are the planets do not show these slight shifts.

Tonatiuh was the eagle-plumed sun god of the Aztecs. The snake he holds in his left hand is the symbol of his omnipotence.

The Earth and its satellite the moon, as they would look from a rocket far in space.

THE EARTH

THE earth is endlessly revolving in space, which makes us all space travelers. It takes us one year to make the complete trip around the sun. (A year is exactly 365 days, six hours, nine minutes, and nine seconds.) In addition the earth turns completely around on itself every day. Traveling at the rate of 18 1/2 miles per second, it traverses each year an orbit that is 600 million miles long. It passes through night and day each twenty-four hours and through four seasons in the course of every year. The reason that we who live on the earth do not even feel ourselves moving is because earth, sea, and sky are traveling with us, all at exactly the same breathtaking speed.

What have we learned over the centuries about this planet that carries us?

Night, day, and local time

The sun never rises, but if we get up early in the morning and look out of our window the sun *appears* to come up from the east, travel across the sky, and finally, in the evening, set in the west.

But what actually happens is quite different. The earth is a ball spinning on an imaginary stick that runs through the middle of it. The imaginary stick is called an *axis*. The spinning is called *rotation*. Each complete spin or rotation takes twenty-four hours. During those twenty-four hours there are certain times when our side of the earth is facing the sun. That is our day. When we are facing away from the sun it is dark, and we are having night.

While we are sleeping under a starry sky, the people on the opposite side of the earth are enjoying the bright noonday sun.

On many world maps you will see lines that go from pole to pole and divide the world into sections, somewhat like an orange. These are called *meridians*. Every point in the world lies within two meridians. As the earth turns and the sun is right above a given meridian, the sun is said to be at its zenith and it is noon there. As the earth turns toward the east, the sun

Soon after men observed that night and day alternated, they also noticed that seasons followed one another in regular succession. This succession of the seasons and the various climates on the Earth's six continents depend upon the angle of inclination of the sun's rays on these continents.

passes over Berlin one hour sooner than it passes over Paris. When it is noon in Berlin it is, therefore, only eleven o'clock in Paris. In the same way ships on the eastern Atlantic see the sun rise hours before it rises in New York.

As soon as traveling became easy, and people no longer told time simply by the sun, these changes of time became very inconvenient, so all the nations of

the world joined together to agree on a universal time system. The globe was re-divided into twenty-four time zones, sectioned off once again like an orange. The first time belt includes Greenwich, England, and the entire belt uses the sun time of the observatory at Greenwich. If we travel east from there, each time belt is one hour ahead; if we travel to the west, each time belt is one hour behind.

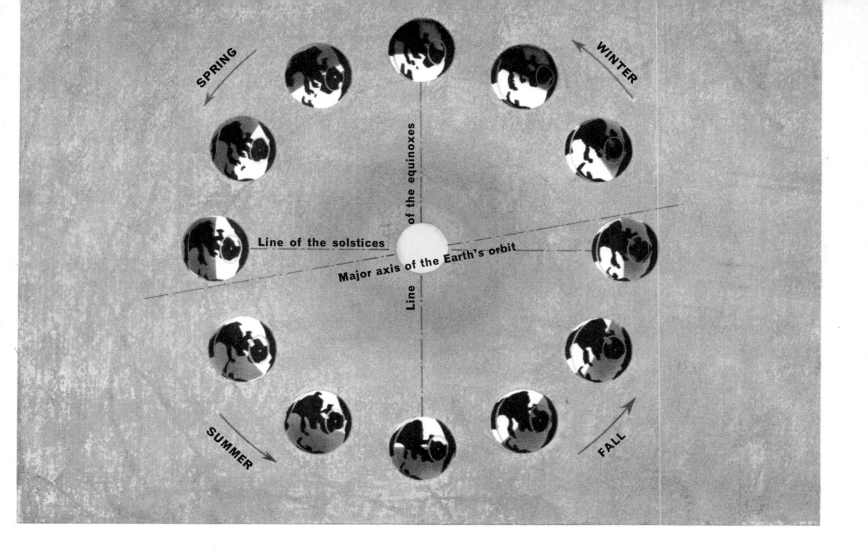

Primitive men learned that time was divided into days and nights. The alternation of day and night is caused by the Earth's movement about its own axis. If the Earth were motionless, half the globe would have perpetual daylight and the other half perpetual night. The Earth turns from west to east, and it is because of this that the sun appears in the east and disappears twelve hours later in the west. Sun time does not use time zones but considers the exact position of the sun. When it is 6:55 A.M. in New York, it is 11:50 A.M. in London, exactly noon in Paris, 12:40 P.M. in Rome, and 9:09 P.M. in Tokyo, sun time.

When it is 7 A.M. Eastern Standard Time in New York, the clock in the Greenwich Observatory is striking noon because there are five time zones between New York and London.

The United States stretches so far from east to west that it includes four time zones. When it is eight o'clock in the morning in Washington, D.C., it is 7 A.M. in Chicago and only 4 A.M. in San Francisco. When two parts of a smaller country extend into different time zones, geographical boundaries are often used instead of meridians to mark off zones.

The seasons

If the axis on which the earth rotates were perpendicular to the plane of its path around the sun, the sun's rays would always fall vertically on the equator and the lighted side of the earth would always extend from the North Pole to the South Pole. There would

be no seasons. Near the equator the climate would be very hot, at the Poles·it would be very cold, with the intermediate regions having climates between these two extremes. Since the weather would never change, the plants and animals of any region would be very different from those now present.

During the 365 days of the earth's orbit, the sun reaches its zenith directly on the equator only twice a year. One such occasion is on March twenty-first. We call that day *spring equinox,* which means "equal night," because all over the world on that day the day and night are exactly twelve hours long. Each day of the following three months the sun appears higher in the sky of the Northern Hemisphere, and the North Pole is in perpetual sunshine. By June twenty-first the entire North Frigid Zone, contained within the Tropic of Capricorn, is in sunshine the full twenty-four hours of the day.

The sun now starts its swing to the south, and on

TIME ZONES

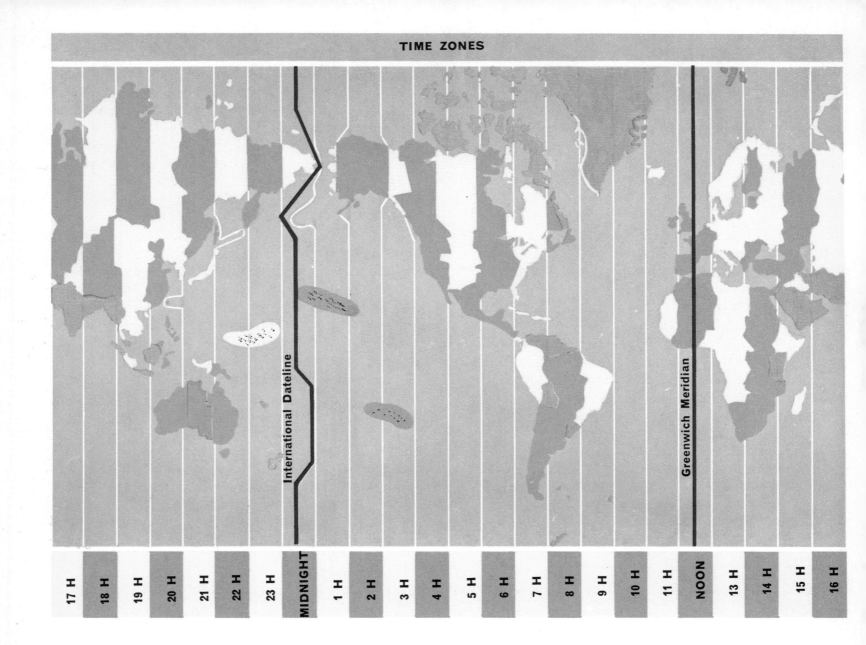

International Dateline

Greenwich Meridian

17 H | 18 H | 19 H | 20 H | 21 H | 22 H | 23 H | MIDNIGHT | 1 H | 2 H | 3 H | 4 H | 5 H | 6 H | 7 H | 8 H | 9 H | 10 H | 11 H | NOON | 13 H | 14 H | 15 H | 16 H

September twenty-first it again is back to the equator it left six months earlier. This is the *autumnal equinox*. The following half-year the process is repeated in the Southern Hemisphere. The North Frigid Zone is in darkness for twenty-four hours while the South Frigid Zone, which is contained within the Tropic of Cancer, has its twenty-four-hour day on the twenty-first of December.

Thus there is always a difference of six months in the seasons of the Northern and Southern Hemispheres. It is caused by the tilt of the earth's axis in relation to the plane of its path about the sun. The hemisphere tilted away from the sun has less sun and, therefore, colder weather. When we have winter the Southern Hemisphere has summer. When we have spring they have fall. When the days are long and hot in New York and Paris, they are short and wintery in Sydney, Australia. When children in North America are trudging to school through banks of snow, children in Brazil are going swimming and enjoying their summer vacation.

Since the beginning of history men have divided the year into four seasons: the time of the blooming of flowers, the time of the hot winds, the time of the slow dying of leaves, and the time of the cold snows. The surest calendar they had consisted of measuring shadows at various times of the year. The sun is the oldest clock.

The calendar

No yearly calendar can be made which can be used for succeeding years without change. It is difficult to divide into equal parts the period between successive coincidence of the rising of a given star with the sun, which is called a *sidereal year*. This period is 365 days, six hours, nine minutes, and nine seconds.

Since earliest times, most calendars have been based on the seasons. To the Egyptians, the start of the Nile floods marked the start of the year. So that it might not be delayed, they cast offerings of food to the god Hapi into the waters. The rise of the Nile flood waters also coincided with the reappearance, after its long absence, of the star Sirius in the eastern sky. The feast of Sothis, the Egyptian name for Sirius, was New Year's Day. Astrologers would claim to "foretell" when this day would be, although they were probably only shrewd calculators. The Romans simply calculated the year in twelve lunar periods or "moons." But they counted fewer than thirty days between one new moon and the next. As a result, the Roman year was too short and there was a time lag in the seasons which made it necessary to change the calendar. The Romans were not especially bothered about these small differences; every now and then the emperor simply declared that he was adding a moon (or month) to that year.

Map of the Time Zones.
Practically all nations have adopted the Greenwich (England) meridian as the point of origin. The system of time zones cuts the Earth into twenty-four equal parts, and each part differs in time from the next adjacent part by one hour. On land, the zone lines are distorted to make the change of time convenient to the people in a given area. Each new day starts at midnight on the international dateline which is on the opposite side of the Earth from Greenwich meridian.

The sun's rays hit us at different angles during the four seasons. From left to right: **Spring, Summer, Autumn, and Winter.**

The first serious attempt to reform the calendar was made by Julius Caesar in 46 B.C. The Julian Calendar, named after him, made the length of the year 365.25 days, or one quarter of a day over 365. The calculation for the calendar had been made by the scientist Hipparchus.

The Julian year was not entirely accurate. The small difference accumulated over the years. By 1582, there was an error of ten days between the official and astronomical date of Easter.

In 1582 Pope Gregory XIII introduced the Gregorian calendar named after him. He decreed that to make up the lost days, Thursday, October 4, 1582, should be immediately followed by Friday, October fifteenth. Clavius, the Jesuit priest who calculated the calendar, concluded that three days should be dropped every four hundred years. This is done by not counting as leap years the years that end a century unless the number is exactly divisible by four hundred. The years 2000 and 2400 will be leap years, but 2100 and 2200 will not be. In this way there will be ninety-seven instead of one hundred leap years every four hundred years.

Despite these amendments the Gregorian year is still twenty-six seconds per year too long. This means that an additional day will have to be dropped every 3,333 years.

America adopted the Gregorian calendar in 1752. Because this caused the dropping of eleven days from the calendar previously used, George Washington's birthday is celebrated on the twenty-second of February, whereas Washington was actually born on the eleventh of February, 1732, according to our present calendar.

Aztec, Sanscrit, Julian, Merovingian calendars. The Julian year (365.25 days) results in one extra day every 130 years when compared with the tropical year (time from one vernal equinox to the next). The difference between the Gregorian year (365.2425 days) and the tropical year is only .0003 days, so that there are only three extra days in every 10,000 years.

According to the ancient Egyptians, the flooding of the Nile was a manifestation of Hapi, father of the gods. This important event was used to mark the beginning of the year. At this time priests threw fruit, cakes, statuettes and sacrificial animals into the Nile as offerings to the god of abundance.

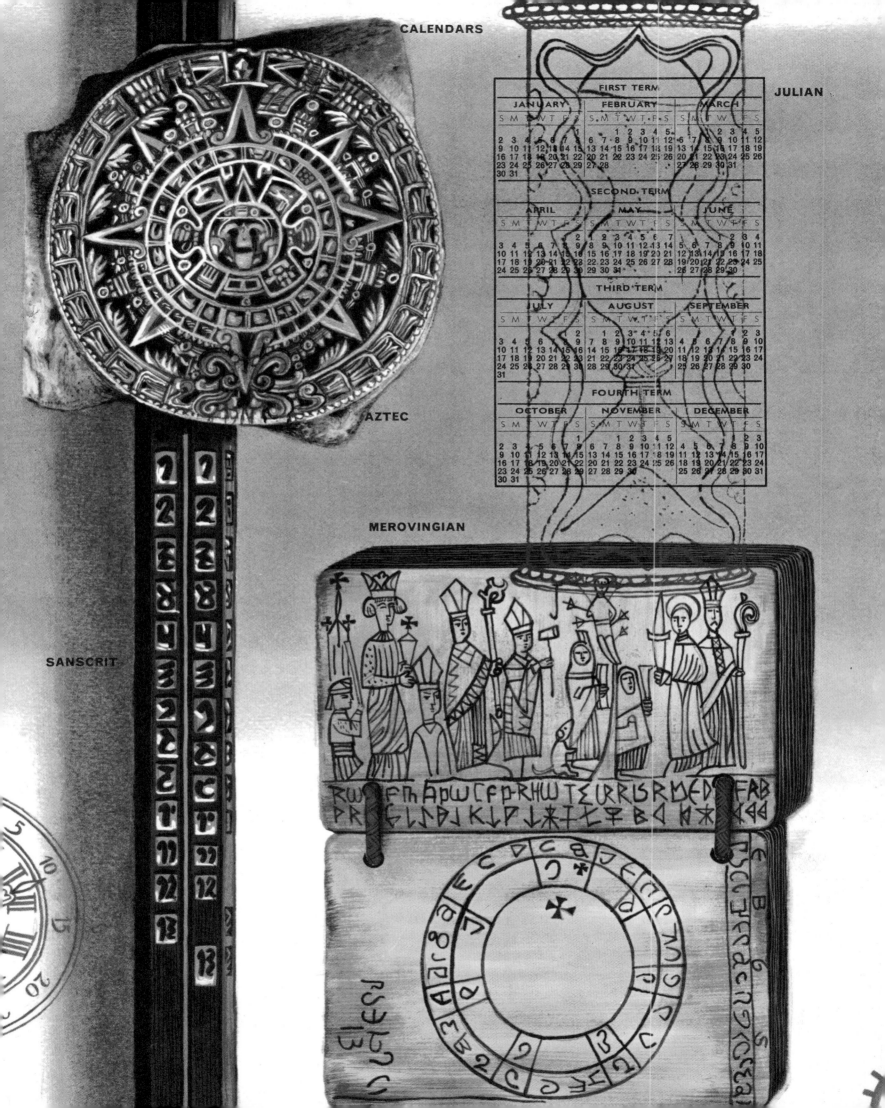

CALENDARS

JULIAN

FIRST TERM		
JANUARY	**FEBRUARY**	**MARCH**
S M T W T F S	S M T W T F S	S M T W T F S
1	1 2 3 4 5	1 2 3 4 5
2 3 4 5 6 7 8	6 7 8 9 10 11 12	6 7 8 9 10 11 12
9 10 11 12 13 14 15	13 14 15 16 17 18 19	13 14 15 16 17 18 19
16 17 18 19 20 21 22	20 21 22 23 24 25 26	20 21 22 23 24 25 26
23 24 25 26 27 28 29	27 28	27 28 29 30 31
30 31		

SECOND TERM		
APRIL	**MAY**	**JUNE**
S M T W T F S	S M T W T F S	S M T W T F S
1 2	1 2 3 4 5 6 7	1 2 3 4
3 4 5 6 7 8 9	8 9 10 11 12 13 14	5 6 7 8 9 10 11
10 11 12 13 14 15 16	15 16 17 18 19 20 21	12 13 14 15 16 17 18
17 18 19 20 21 22 23	22 23 24 25 26 27 28	19 20 21 22 23 24 25
24 25 26 27 28 29 30	29 30 31	26 27 28 29 30

THIRD TERM		
JULY	**AUGUST**	**SEPTEMBER**
S M T W T F S	S M T W T F S	S M T W T F S
1 2	1 2 3 4 5 6	1 2 3
3 4 5 6 7 8 9	7 8 9 10 11 12 13	4 5 6 7 8 9 10
10 11 12 13 14 15 16	14 15 16 17 18 19 20	11 12 13 14 15 16 17
17 18 19 20 21 22 23	21 22 23 24 25 26 27	18 19 20 21 22 23 24
24 25 26 27 28 29 30	28 29 30 31	25 26 27 28 29 30
31		

FOURTH TERM		
OCTOBER	**NOVEMBER**	**DECEMBER**
S M T W T F S	S M T W T F S	S M T W T F S
1	1 2 3 4 5	1 2 3
2 3 4 5 6 7 8	6 7 8 9 10 11 12	4 5 6 7 8 9 10
9 10 11 12 13 14 15	13 14 15 16 17 18 19	11 12 13 14 15 16 17
16 17 18 19 20 21 22	20 21 22 23 24 25 26	18 19 20 21 22 23 24
23 24 25 26 27 28 29	27 28 29 30	25 26 27 28 29 30 31
30 31		

AZTEC

MEROVINGIAN

SANSCRIT

Artemis, the ancient Greek moon goddess, was known as Diana the Huntress to the Romans. She was often pictured either with the crescent moon or a stag.

OUR NEIGHBOR: THE MOON

THE moon is the earth's satellite. It accompanies us on our yearly orbit around the sun while circling around us at the same time. By comparison with other sky distances, the moon is very close to us, only a quarter of a million miles away. If every mile of railroad track in America were laid end to end it would reach the moon, and we could make the trip by train!

In very, very ancient times, cave men worshiped the moon, the ghostly goddess who glowed at night. We now know that the moon's glow comes from the sun's light shining on it. It has no light of its own.

We see only one side of the moon; the other side is always turned away from us. For a long time men thought that the moon did not rotate on its own axis. We now know that the moon does rotate, but its rotation and orbital movement are so synchronized that only one side of it faces us continually. If it did not rotate we would see its other side. Legends have long been invented about the mysterious "other face" of the moon. Cameras mounted in a Russian rocket have photographed this other face, so that astronomers now have some knowledge of its appearance.

It takes the moon 29 1/2 days to travel around the world. To us on Earth the moon seems to be moving across the sky each night. Once again it is the earth's rotation on its axis that produces the apparent motion of the moon. The moon's motion in its orbit about the earth plays a very small part in the apparent motion.

Why are there moonless nights every month?

Because each day the moon "comes up" fifty minutes later than the day before. The earth makes a complete rotation every twenty-four hours. With respect to the apparent motion of the stars across the sky, the moon seems to slip behind. In its orbit about the earth it moves eastward.

Hence, from Earth, we see the moon rise at night for two weeks, but the next two weeks we do not see it for it rises in our sky during the day.

The phases of the moon

The moon does not always look the same in the sky. The different shapes the moon appears to have within a month are called *the phases of the moon*. When the moon passes between us and the sun, its illuminated face is turned away from the earth. The face we see is thus in shadow—a "new" moon we call it. We can hardly see it. Sometimes we are tempted to say: "There is no moon tonight."

The moon proceeds on its orbital course. Gradually we begin to see the part of the moon that is illuminated. This appears as a thin crescent. Every night the lighted area grows larger, and the moon reaches its first quarter when it has covered a quarter of its orbit from its new moon position. We can now see half the face of the moon clearly outlined.

The moon grows still more round. When it has completed half its orbit, we see a "full moon." The surface illuminated by the sun becomes completely visible and the moon is a beautiful shining disk in the heavens.

Then the process begins in reverse; the lighted portion visible from the earth decreases each night. We see a new crescent after we have seen the half-moon of the last quarter.

This crescent is different from the first. To tell whether the crescent is that of the first part of the moon's cycle or the last add a bar to the crescent. If it forms a *b* you know it is a "baby" moon, but if it forms a *d* you know it is a "dying" moon.

In its last phase the moon is again between the sun and the earth. It disappears in its own shadow. The cycle is about to start again, for another 29 1/2 days. The period between two new moons is called a *lunation*.

If you want to observe the moon, the best time to do it is the period from the last quarter to the first quarter. At that time there is the least glare from the sun. Even small telescopes or binoculars are enough to show craters and mountains which, during this period, are set off from the rocky landscape by very deep shadows.

Eclipses of the moon

Eclipses of the moon terrified our distant ancestors just as much as did eclipses of the sun. A shadow passed across the glowing moon and sometimes covered it completely. What could explain this strange phenomenon?

Like all solid bodies in a light, the earth casts a shadow. Since our planet is a sphere, this shadow is cone-shaped. It comes to a point like an elongated artillery shell, a shell that is a million miles long. Since the moon is never more than a quarter of a million miles away from the earth, it may during its course pass through the shadow of the earth.

If it passes through the center of the earth's shadow, the eclipse will be total. If, on the other hand, only part of the moon enters the dark cone, the eclipse will be partial.

During a total eclipse the moon may become completely invisible. But we can sometimes see it faintly illuminated by a reddish light. This is because the lower layers of the atmosphere allow only the red rays of the sun to pass through them.

An eclipse of the moon is visible in all areas of the earth in which the moon is above the horizon.

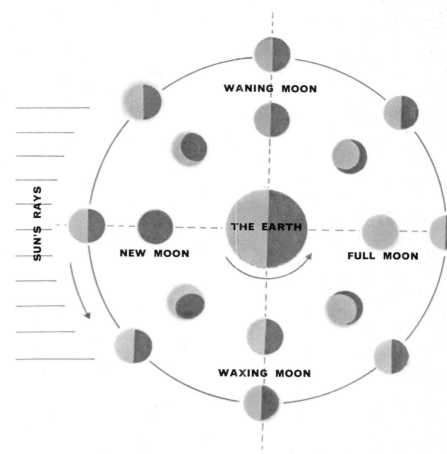

The phases of the moon are the different ways the moon is visible from the Earth during the 29 days and 13 hours of its revolution. The inner circle on the diagram represents the moon's phases as seen from the Earth. The outer circle represents the moon's position in space.

◀ As the drawing shows, the moon's equator would encircle only four-fifths of Europe.

The tides

The moon exerts a considerable attraction on the earth. Although this attraction is very weak compared to that of the sun, the moon is so close to us that it does have a definite effect in producing tides on the earth's surface.

The sun's attraction also produces tides. But though enormous by comparison with the moon, the sun, at 93 million miles, is so distant that the tidal effect it produces is less than half of that of the moon.

When the sun and the moon are in line with the earth, their effects in producing tides are combined. These tides, which we call spring tides, are very high. At other times, when the moon and the sun are not in line, the tides are lower. These are known as neap tides.

A theory has been advanced that there were once a number of moons. According to this theory, millions of years ago there were other moons in our sky which drew nearer and nearer to the earth. They may have disappeared by crashing into our planet or have disappeared in space. According to this bold and interesting theory, one of these moons came

In a few years, mankind will build its first station on the surface of the moon. The materials, mainly plastics, will be made on Earth and transported to the moon by rockets so large we can hardly imagine them today. The first problem our explorers will need to overcome is lack of air. Most of the designs now being studied call for completely airtight installations with plants generating an artificial atmosphere.

We now think that the first astronauts to explore the moon will use a sort of robot-cabin combined with a spacesuit. It will be powered by independent batteries and will be pressurized. Part of its equipment will consist of:

1. Radio antenna
2. Position and signaling lights
3. Photographic and television cameras
4. Transparent panoramic helmet
5. Geologist's hammer (for sampling the moon's surface)
6. Flare pistol
7. Weighted boots

The first men who land on the moon will see a beautiful object in the sky—the Earth.

close to our earth and exerted an enormous attraction on our seas. The tides were very high, so high that they spilled many hundreds of miles over the land.

Why are the huge cliffs in the Cordilleras scarred right up to their summits by deep indentations as if they were marks of former high tides? Why are the waters of Lake Titicaca salty? Perhaps millions of years ago, "dead" moons approaching the earth forced the tides to be so high that the whole lake was submerged.

Under the moon's attraction the ocean layer swells slightly and becomes oval in shape. This attraction of the water from one section of the globe lowers the level of waters lapping other continents.

As the moon moves westward, the wave of water (the tide) moves in the same direction. The moon crosses the coast; the water beats against the cliffs and covers the beaches. We say it is *high tide.*

The moon continues on its course. It moves farther beyond the coast and the waters recede. Roughly six hours later, when the moon is halfway on the course to the other side of the world, the water drops at the foot of the cliffs and the beaches are completely dry, and we say it is *low tide.*

While the waters facing the moon are bulging, the waters on the opposite side of the earth bulge, too. That is because the moon also attracts the earth and the earth pulls away from the waters. The waters, as if left behind, collect into a bulge and form another high tide. That is why during the twenty-four-hour rotation we get two high tides. The waters between the bulges are meanwhile at low tide.

Let's go to the moon

Let's take the next rocket to the moon and see for ourselves what it's like there.

When we land, our spaceship lands on its tail. We get out, dressed in our spacesuits and provided with bottles of oxygen, because the moon has no atmosphere. Atmosphere is the dusty, gaseous layer that scatters the sun's rays and provides us with "sky light." If the moon were also enveloped in atmosphere, we would see its outlines from Earth as vague and gauzy. Since we see its edges so clearly we deduce that it has no atmosphere. So, even if we land in full day, the sky around us is pitch black and filled with stars which shine and sparkle far more brightly than they do from Earth. A greenish crescent shining over a mountain range is the earth. We talk in signs, since there is no air to carry sound waves. Our ears can hardly get accustomed to the absolute silence all around us.

We start walking. Our equipment should weigh us down but it feels extraordinarily light.

The moon is fifty times smaller than the earth, but its mass is 1/83 of that of our planet and its pull of gravity is six times less. If you weigh 120 pounds on Earth, you would weigh only twenty pounds on the moon. If you were to jump in the air, a jump that would carry you one yard on Earth would carry you six yards on the moon. An Olympic pole vaulter would have no trouble vaulting over a hill.

A cooling system helps us endure the almost two-hundred-degree heat. We walk under a blinding sun

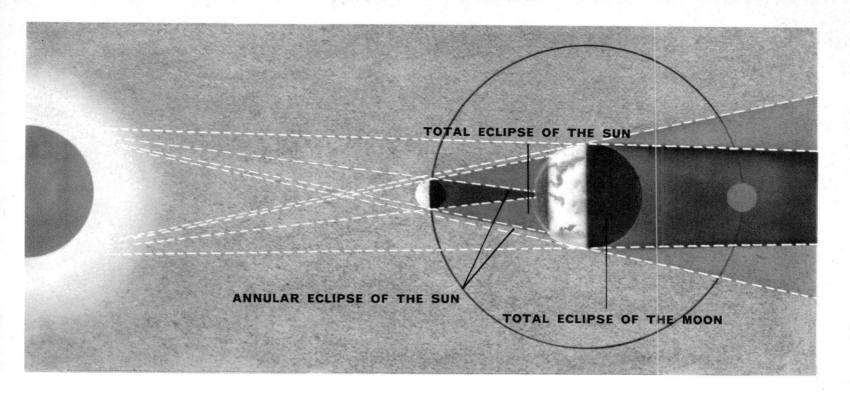

Eclipses of the moon and the sun. Solar eclipses: A total eclipse occurs when the apparent diameter of the moon is greater than that of the sun (the moon being very close to the Earth); an eclipse is known as annular when the apparent diameter of the moon is smaller than the sun (as when the moon is at the apogee of its orbit); eclipses are considered partial when the moon blocks off only part of the sun. A total lunar eclipse (far right) occurs when the moon passes through the Earth's shadow.

whose rays yield a bluish light. The landscape is desertlike and the shadows are dark and deep. As far as we can see, mountains and their jagged peaks line the horizon. Seen this closely, the craters with which we had become familiar in the telescope are not recognizable. We pull out our maps and try to determine where we are. The earliest-seen craters were named after scientists. But which is Leibnitz? Which Plato? Which Copernicus?

Some of these craters have a diameter of 150 *miles* and they are as deep as the Pacific. The Newton crater is more than *six thousand* yards deep.

High and low tides are the effect of the gravitational pull of the sun and moon on the oceans. When the gravitational pull of the sun and moon coincide, flood tides occur. (Earth, moon and sun are on the same line.) Neap tides occur when the sun and the moon are not in the same line. At this time the lines connecting the Earth with the sun, and the Earth with the moon, form a right angle, with the Earth at the apex. In certain parts of the world, the gravitational pull of the sun has a greater influence than that of the moon. This may be observed in Tahiti and on Tuesday Island, about 15 miles off the coast of Australia.

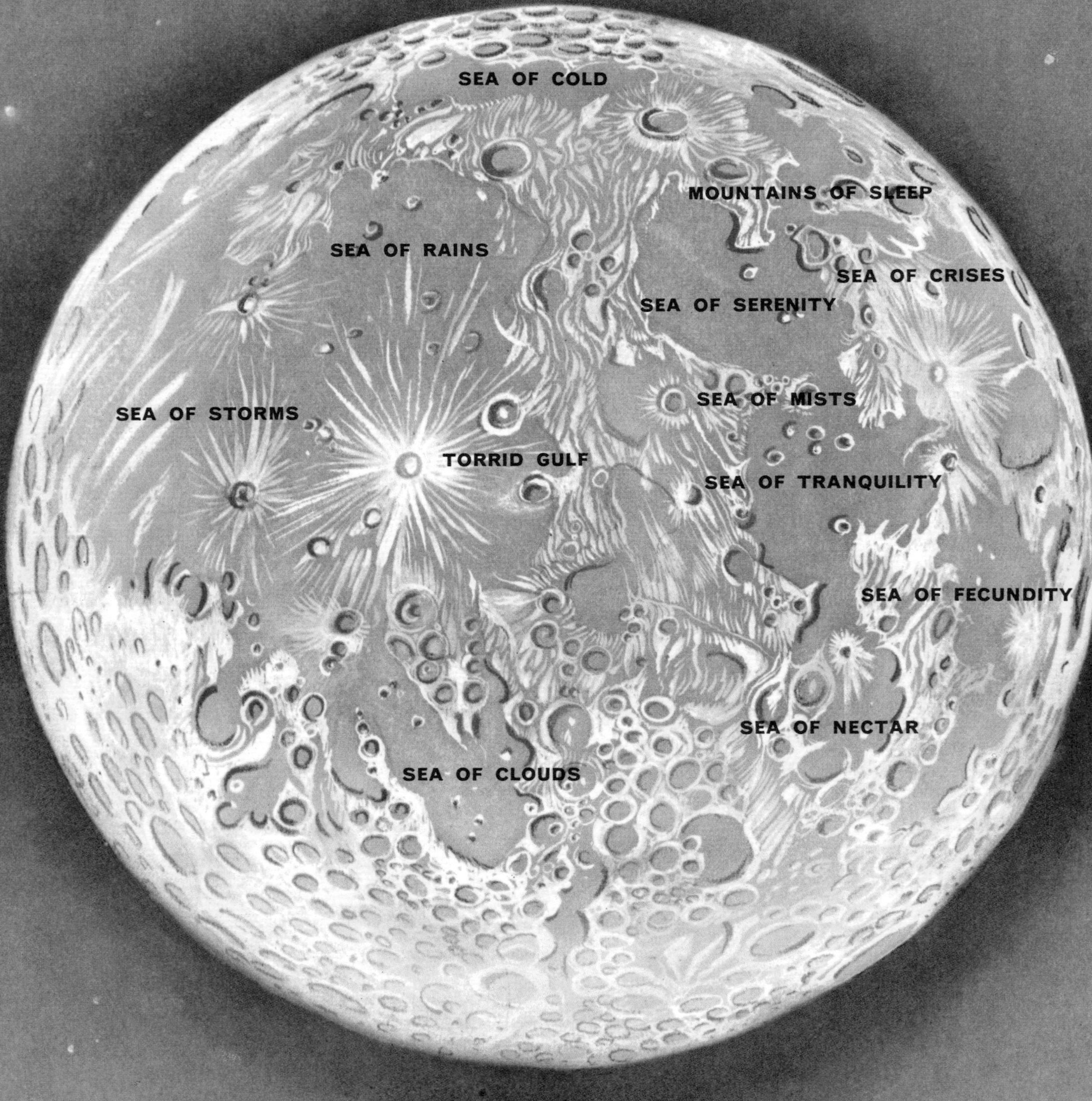

SEA OF COLD

MOUNTAINS OF SLEEP

SEA OF RAINS

SEA OF CRISES

SEA OF SERENITY

SEA OF STORMS

SEA OF MISTS

TORRID GULF

SEA OF TRANQUILITY

SEA OF FECUNDITY

SEA OF NECTAR

SEA OF CLOUDS

Above: **The visible half of the moon as photographed by all the great observatories on Earth.**

On the right: **A drawing of the unseen half, derived from photographs taken by Lunik II (1959). The cameras were triggered from Russia while the satellite was 292,000 miles from the Earth and 43,500 miles from the moon. This remarkable technical achievement proved that the shape of the moon is spherical, and also showed that the topography of the hidden side is less contorted than that of the visible half. (The Arabic numerals indicate the craters, mountains, and seas never before seen. The Roman numerals indicate the areas astronomers had already plotted.)**

I. THE HUMBOLDT SEA	VI. THE SEA OF FECUNDITY	4. THE TZIOLOVSKI CRATER
II. THE SEA OF CRISES	VII. THE SOUTHERN SEA	5. THE LOMONOSSOV CRATER
III. THE REGIONAL SEA	1. SEA OF MOSCOW	6. THE JOLIOT-CURIE CRATER
IV. THE SEA OF WAVES	2. BAY OF THE ASTRONAUTS	7. THE SOVIET MOUNTAINS
V. THE SMITH SEA	3. PART OF THE SOUTHERN SEA	8. THE SEA OF DREAMS
(300 miles in diameter)	(the rest is in the visible half of the moon)	

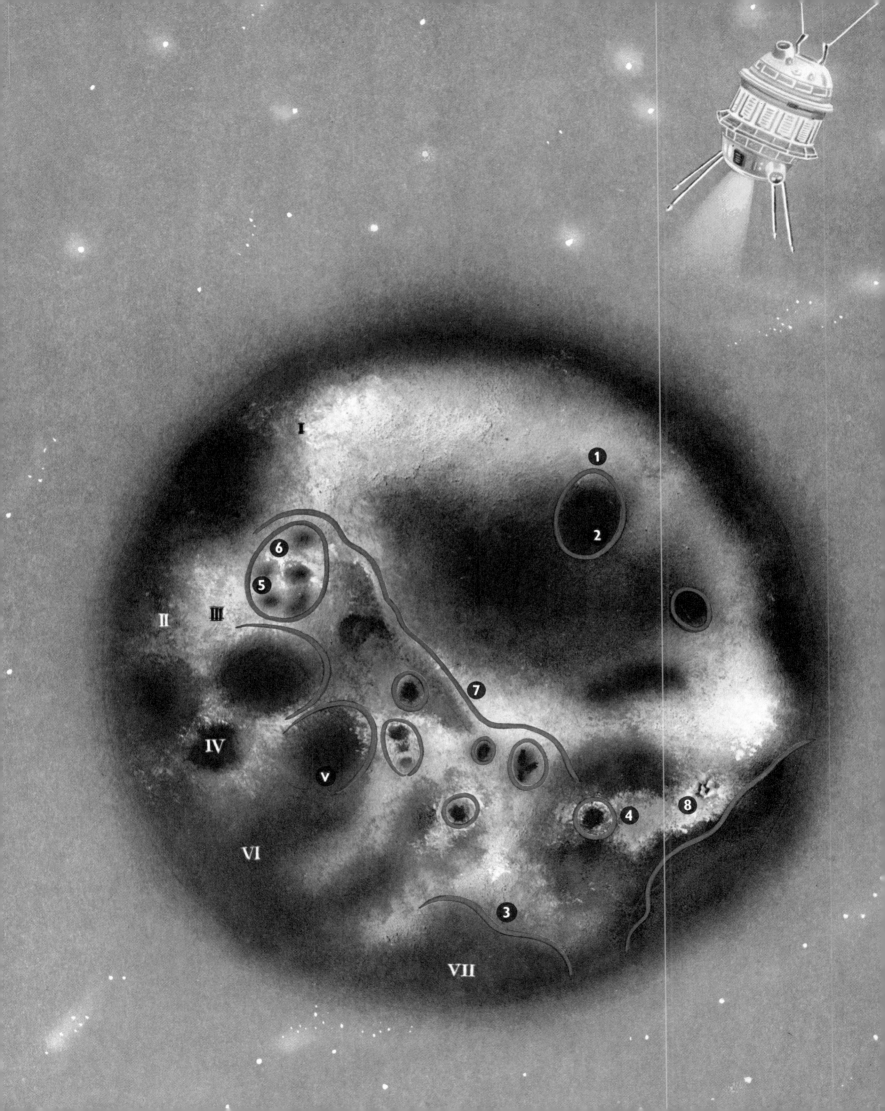

Lunik II took only 3 days to travel the 238,000 miles separating the moon from the Earth. To make this same trip, a Boeing 707 cruising at 535 mph would require 19 days, while a train traveling at 95 mph would need 3 1/2 months and a car speeding along at 85 mph, 3 months and 24 days. A race horse would have to gallop at 35 mph for 11 months, and a man on a bicycle would have to pedal a fast 20 mph for 15 months. As for a pedestrian, even at 6 mph it would take him 4 years and 5 months to reach the moon.

How these craters came to be is not yet known. We don't know whether they are dead volcanoes, or holes made by falling meteors. If we walk around one of these craters, which we saw from the earth as a gray spot and for years wrongly called a sea, we will find ourselves in a desert of pebbles and dust. Early moon observers have given these "seas" lovely names: the Sea of Clouds (although there never is a cloud on the moon), the Sea of Rain (although no rain has ever dropped on this desert), the Sea of Serenity, and the Sea of Tranquility.

After two weeks we will have to return to Earth, even if our oxygen supply is still ample, for two weeks of night will be beginning.

Because of the way the moon rotates, a day on the moon is the length of fourteen Earth days. A month on the moon consists of fourteen Earth days of bluish light and fourteen days of total darkness and freezing cold (112° F. below zero).

Eating dinner by "Earth light"—the sun's light reflected to the moon by the earth—might sound romantic, but it would also be very cold. It is easier to air-condition the spaceship against the heat of day than to heat it against the cold. But in two weeks we would have learned a great deal. With the tele-scopes and cameras that we brought along we would have photographed the skies far more clearly than we can through the earth's atmosphere. We would have learned more about the earth's atmosphere by seeing it from the outside. We would have done a great deal to prepare for future operations. Perhaps by exploring the mountains, called "rills," we would have found that in their shadows men can endure the heat of day without being bothered by bulky spacesuits. We would have collected many rock samples and dust samples to take back to geologists who stayed behind. These would tell us whether meteors exploded on the face of the moon and formed those mysterious craters. We would have studied every kind of radiation, and in less serious moments we would simply enjoy all the new sensations of this desert-world.

When men reach the moon, the shelters that will house them will have to be dug underground. They will be heated, ventilated, and air-conditioned. Men living in these space stations will need to wear their spacesuits only when they come to the surface. We are just beginning to know the other side of the moon, from photographs made by the first rocket to circle the moon. Perhaps we will live to see mining compan-ies open for business there!

We board our spaceship and prepare to blast off. Below, our footprints look eerie in the otherwise wild and barren landscape. With no rain to wash them away and no wind to disturb them they will still be there when we come back.

Our spaceship begins its journey back to Earth. We look out of our porthole and watch the moon grow smaller and smaller behind us. Soon the immense plain called the Sea of Storms, almost half the size of the United States, once more looks like a grain of sand on the surface of the glowing disk. Then we will turn our thoughts away from the moon and back to our own planet, Earth. Our main rocket will put us on a path that will bring us into Earth's gravitational field and into orbit. After that we will have two choices. Either we can maneuver our spaceship so that it meets with an orbiting space station where we can transfer our men and equipment for the last stage of our journey, or we can use the re-entry methods already tested by our fellow astronauts. This will mean adjusting our spaceship in orbit until the retro-rockets can be fired at just the right time and then floating down by parachute into the arms of our eager countrymen.

The first man-made objects to explore the moon will undoubtedly be automated tanks, radio-controlled from Earth or from an intermediate space station. Naturally such tanks will be equipped with radar and television cameras.

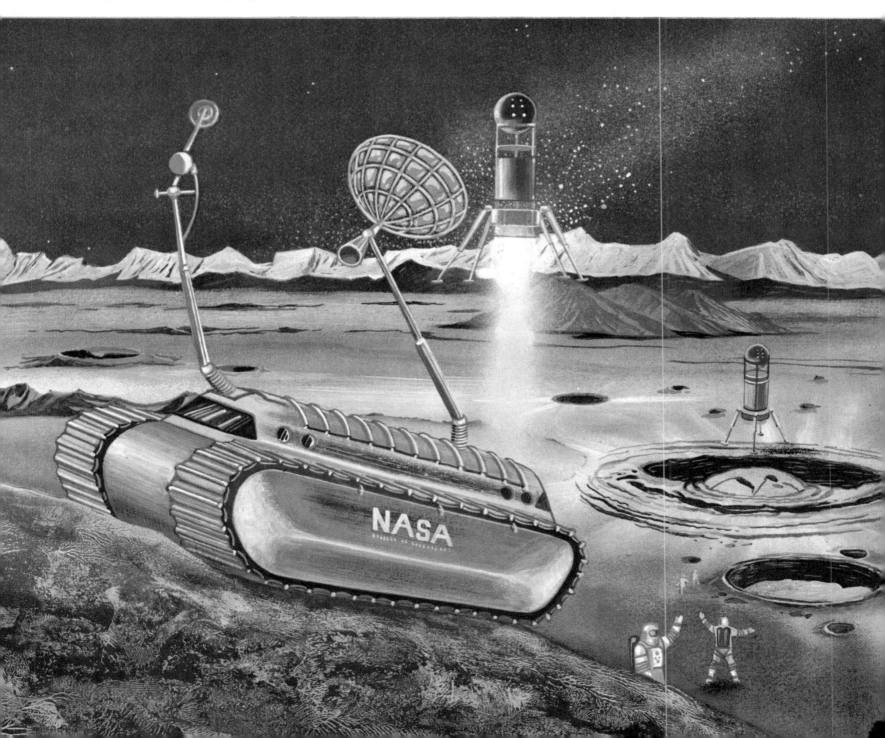

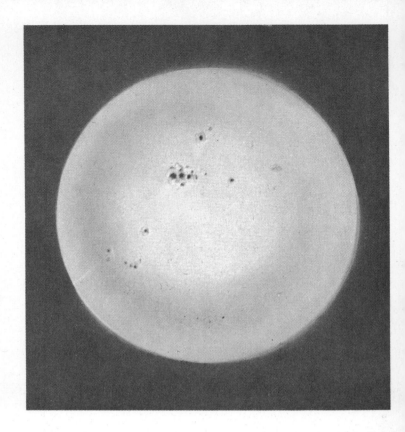

Left: **Solar flares, as seen during an annular eclipse of the sun.**

Right: **Galileo was the first to see spots on the sun's surface in 1610. Close observation of the comings and goings of sunspots proved to astronomers that the sun was a sphere and that its period of rotation was about 27 days.**

THE SUN

OUR sun, the center of our solar system, is completely different from any of the planets that circle around it.

Of all the bodies in the heavens, next to the earth, we are most interested in the sun because we know that it provides us with heat, light, and energy. And all this despite the fact that we receive only two billionths of the sun's rays. The rest are dispersed in space. This tiny portion of the sun's energy is all we need to maintain life on Earth.

The sun is 25,000 light-years from the center of our galaxy. It makes up part of the movement of our galaxy by turning around the center of gravity of the galaxy every 220 million years. The sun is only an average-sized star, much smaller than millions of others. Nevertheless it is huge compared to the earth. It would take a million earths to make up a sun. The sun's diameter is 109 times as large as ours.

The mass of the sun is so great that the gravitational attraction at the surface of the sun is almost thirty times the gravitational attraction at the surface of the earth. We said before that a man weighing 120 pounds on Earth would weigh twenty pounds on the moon. That same man would weigh almost two tons on the sun; a pendulum clock ticking once each second on Earth would tick six times each second on the sun.

Several observatories in different parts of the world observe the sun every day. They see a strange sight. The shape of the sun seems to change; its edges are always moving. Instead of being a smooth, even color, the surface appears to have a grainy texture. Despite the fact that it is 93 million miles away, we can clearly see this granulation. This must mean that each "grain" is the size of the state of Arizona.

In other, non-grainy sections of the sun, we see spots that are bigger and darker than the grains. Calculations tell us that these spots are at least five times the diameter of the earth. Observation of the sun has shown us that these sunspots change over the years. Some years they disappear altogether and others they appear in great number. For five or six years they will constantly increase, and for the next five or six they diminish. The same cycle repeats every eleven years. This proves that the sun is a variable star which does not always give off the same amount of light or heat.

The temperature at the sun's surface is about

six thousand degrees Centigrade or eleven *thousand* degrees Fahrenheit. Inside it is certainly many millions of degrees. Such intensity of heat could not come from mere burning, so scientists have deduced that it must come from atomic energy. Atomic explosions, continually taking place on the sun, must change hydrogen atoms to helium atoms and thus produce the fantastic heat. Spectroscope studies of the sun have shown that the sun has most of the metals that exist on Earth, all in a gaseous state, but its mass is principally made up of hydrogen and helium. When hydrogen fuses to form helium, tongues of flame called *prominences* shoot into the *chromosphere*, the sun's atmosphere, which stretches for many thousands of miles around it. Some of these prominences shoot out farther from the sun than twice the distance between the earth and the moon.

A second thinner layer of atmosphere, called the *corona*, stretches around the chromosphere. Although the chromosphere is a lighter mixture of hydrogen, helium, calcium, and iron, the gas is highly ionized and gives a different spectrum from the surface of the sun.

Eclipses of the sun

The moon also throws a conical shadow, but it is far smaller than that of the earth. If the moon is to hide the sun, the cone will have to touch part of the earth. Under the most favorable conditions, the patch cast on the earth's surface by the conical shadow is 170 miles in diameter.

Thus eclipses of the sun are not visible at every point on the globe, but only in the area on which the patch of shadow falls. Furthermore, eclipses of the sun are very short. Since the moon is moving at about thirty-five miles per minute, its shadow will move very quickly across the earth's surface.

Eclipses of the sun are total, annular, or partial. The eclipse will be total when the moon completely covers the sun. It is annular when the shadow cone is too short to reach the earth. At that time the sun will appear as a bright ring surrounding the black disk of the moon. The eclipse is partial when the moon covers one side of the sun.

The Chaldeans in the sixth century B.C. had already calculated the period between the recurrent appearances of eclipses. It is called the Saros and covers eighteen years and eleven days. It represents 223 lunations. At the end of this period, the sun and the moon having returned to the same positions in the heavens, the eclipse phenomena recur in the same sequence.

Solar eclipses are of great scientific interest. They enable us to study the composition of our sun, its flaming corona and its ring of projecting flames. Since eclipses are usually very brief, astronomers undertake long journeys to distant lands to observe the phenomenon.

Solar Eclipses (from left to right): **a total eclipse; an annular eclipse; a partial eclipse.** The eclipse is total when the apparent diameter of the moon is equal to or greater than the apparent diameter of the sun. The eclipse is annular when the apparent diameter of the moon is less than the apparent diameter of the sun.

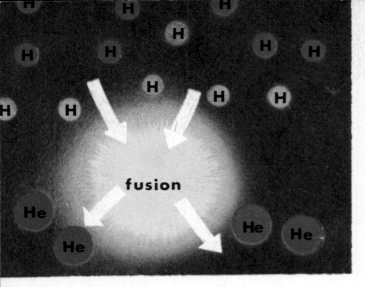

fusion

The sun is our greatest source of energy. Solar energy is the result of innumerable thermonuclear reactions. Every split second, millions of hydrogen atoms (H) are thrown together at incredible speeds, and these atoms unite (nuclear fusion) to form atoms of helium (He). The light and energy resulting from these reactions radiate from all parts of the sun's surface. In a few tens of billions of years, the sun will explode and become a super-nova. The sun's sphere will expand and swallow one by one all the planets of the solar system, with the possible exceptions of Uranus, Neptune, and Pluto. Scientists believe, though, that about ten billion years from today, when the sun has used up roughly one-third of its present hydrogen supply, life on this planet as we know it will be long dead, and the oceans will begin to boil on Earth's parched shell.

How big is the sun? Its diameter is 109 times that of the Earth and its mass is 330,000 times greater. An object would weigh 28 times as much on the surface of the sun as it would on Earth. An average man weighing 160 pounds would tip the scales at over two tons (if he were not burned up first — the surface temperature of the sun is about 11,000°F.). Light from the sun traveling at 186,000 miles per second takes 8 minutes and 18 seconds to cover the 93 million miles which separate it from our planet. Without the sun's light and warmth, the Earth would be but a dead planet, a spherical ice cube floating in space.

Solar flares are red and gold masses of flaming gas which leap out from the chromosphere, occasionally to heights of 500,000 miles or 63 times the diameter of the Earth. They can assume varied forms—waves, curls, eddies, etc. Some solar flares may last for months while others, like geyserflares, resemble jets of flame or fountains of fire which eventually lose themselves in space.

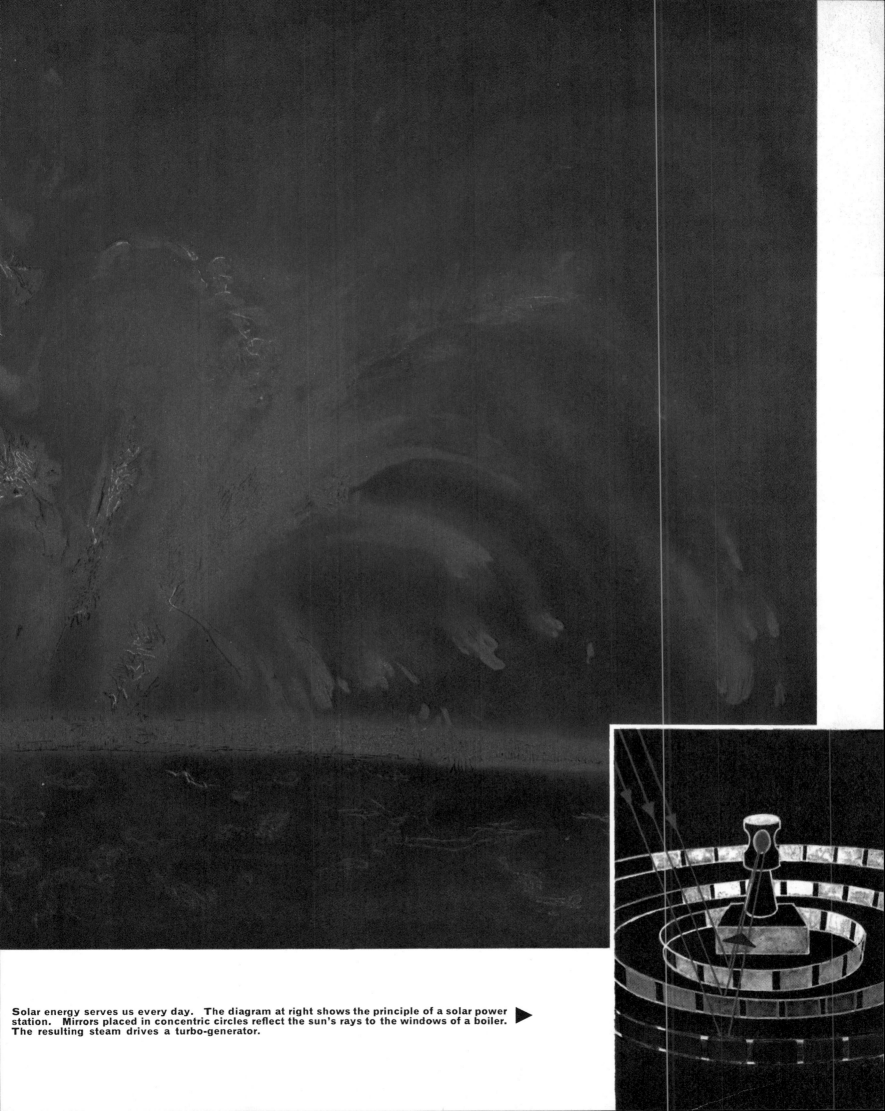

Solar energy serves us every day. The diagram at right shows the principle of a solar power station. Mirrors placed in concentric circles reflect the sun's rays to the windows of a boiler. The resulting steam drives a turbo-generator. ▶

As early as the third century B.C., a Greek astronomer, Aristarchus of Samos, stated that the earth moved in an orbit about the sun. It was not until the beginning of the sixteenth century, however, that the Polish astronomer Copernicus restated the idea of a sun-centered system which included the other planets as well as Earth.

The planets then known were Mercury, Venus, Earth, Mars, Jupiter, and Saturn. According to Copernicus, the orbits of these heavenly bodies were circles.

In 1609, Kepler, a German scientist, proved that the planets traveled in ellipses and not in circles, and that the sun was a common focus for all the elliptical paths of the planets. He also established that the times taken to complete the orbits depended upon the planets' distances from the sun, the farthest out taking the longest time.

THE PLANETS OF THE SOLAR SYSTEM

God distributing the planets, from a twelfth century mosaic on the dome of the church at Montreale, in Sicily.

Mercury

This planet, the nearest to the sun, would not be a pleasant world for us to live on. Just as the moon, in revolving, keeps the same face toward the earth, Mercury always keeps the same face toward the sun. This side has continual burning day—900° F., or hotter than a blast furnace—while the other has continual night and deadly cold—450° below zero. Standing in the twilight zone where you might still be able to stand the temperature, you would need dark goggles to protect your eyes, for the blazing sun appears three times bigger than it does on Earth. Because Mercury has little or no atmosphere to diffuse the sun's light, you would see the sun burning against a black sky.

Mercury is the fastest traveling of the planets. It makes its orbit around the sun in eighty-eight days. To us it always appears very near the sun and for that reason we see it best just before sunrise or at sunset, when the sun's rays do not hide it from our view. From Earth we see Mercury, like the moon, going through phases: crescent, half, and full. It glows a bright yellow-orange.

Half as wide as the earth, Mercury is much lighter and therefore has a very low gravity. A person weighing a hundred pounds on Earth would weigh a scant twenty-seven on Mercury.

Photographs of the spots on Mercury have enabled astrophysicists to show that the surface of this planet is much like the moon's. According to them, the surface of Mercury is also covered by extremely fine granular dust. Because of its low gravity and high temperature on the hot side, it is unable to hold a gas.

From what we can tell of Mercury, it is a planet of extremes. Not only is it the fastest moving, but it has both the hottest and coldest temperatures. The lack of atmosphere prevents the heat and cold from being spread around. The lack of water prevents any food from growing. This little world, for Mercury is also the smallest planet, must be nothing but a barren wasteland.

Venus

Next to the sun and the moon, Venus is the brightest "star" in the sky. But we never see it during the night. It seems to follow the sun in its course. It appears in the twilight of sunset, or at dawn. It is thus called both the *Evening Star* and the *Morning Star*.

Venus is the planet most like ours in size. Its diameter is 7,600 miles, slightly less than our own. On Venus we would weigh the same as we do on Earth.

Like Mars and the moon, Venus has phases. They can be observed with even small binoculars.

It orbits at 67 million miles from the sun. It takes about 225 days to complete its orbit. In its course it passes in front of the sun (where we can best observe it) far less frequently than does Mercury—only once every 120 years. The next time will be on the seventh of June, 2004.

The United States spacecraft *Mariner II* has provided us with additional information about the planet. We know that it rotates very slowly, so that the same side is exposed to the sun for long periods. One day on Venus may be the length of 225 Earth days. Since Venus is closer to the sun than is Earth, the surface temperature is much higher—approximately 800° F.

Atmospheric pressure on Venus is far greater than it is on our planet. The atmosphere appears to consist mostly of nitrogen and carbon dioxide, indicating that there is little plant life using up carbon dioxide and

The surface of Venus is hidden by a thick blanket of clouds, and before the journey of the United States spacecraft Mariner II, scientists had widely differing theories about what the planet was like. They thought it might be a burning desert swept by fiery winds, or an ocean sprinkled with islands. A third theory suggested that it was covered by a jungle of ferns and shrubs. We are certain now, however, that plant life as we know it could not exist there.

releasing oxygen into the air. All of these conditions —the high temperature, the great pressure, the content of the air—make it impossible that human beings like ourselves could live there.

Mars

This is our nearest major planet neighbor. Every seventeen years Mars reaches a point when it is closest to Earth: 35 million miles. The next time a journey could be most easily made would be in 1973. Astronauts will undoubtedly make the journey soon and perhaps at last clear up the legends and theories about Martian people that have existed on Earth for centuries.

We know that Mars is a small planet that glows with a reddish light. It orbits the sun in 687 days. Its own rotation is twenty-four hours and thirty-seven minutes which makes the Martian day almost exactly like ours.

Mars also has seasons, but longer than our own. Its year is twice the length of ours.

Mars probably has some atmosphere. We have detected oxygen and water vapor. Yellowish fogs and even clouds move around the planet.

During its winter, we see both poles of Mars as shining white. In summer these apparent ice caps melt and the white patches disappear almost completely. The rest of the surface shows large pink or orange patches and surfaces of a deeper color. These patches turn from yellow to green during the course of the seasons. Are they areas of vegetation?

The theory that the white lines that appear to crisscross Mars were dug by the Martians to irrigate the deserts has been abandoned. These canals were thought to carry streams of water to the Martian equator from the melting glaciers forming the white patches at the poles.

Now, however, the melting of the two ice patches has been observed. It lasts barely fifteen days. It is hardly likely that the melting water would suffice to fill the lakes and canals.

Further, the density of the water vapor on Mars is only one twentieth of that of our earth's atmosphere. Its oxygen is very rarefied.

This does not, however, prove that Mars is not inhabited. It very probably contains forms of life which differ so greatly from our own that we are unable to picture them, even with the help of the enormous strides science is continually making. We can no more do so than a fish in the very depths of the Pacific can picture a man passing overhead in a ship.

We do not know, either, the stage of civilization reached by any inhabitants of "outer space." How far have they advanced in science, in technique? What fabulous machines have they invented? How long ago? We can only imagine....

The recently discovered Dead Sea Scrolls, written in the first century A.D., speak of a terrible battle. They speak particularly of a weapon that burned more than fire does. The description sounds very much like an atomic explosion.

Inhabitants of other worlds could certainly have acquired, long before us, an astonishing degree of scientific knowledge. Why should we, who are about to embark on space travel, doubt it? There is no reason why Earth should be the only planet in the solar system to have inhabitants. Nor would it have been impossible for space travelers from Mars to land on our planet. But how would they have taken off again? Scientists have thought the answer to that might lie in the mystery of the giant terraces of Baalbek, in the Lebanon Mountains of Syria. Perhaps they were built by space travelers. A single step of the terraces leading up to the platform is made of a piece of dressed stone seventy feet long and 13.6 feet high and weighs over two thousand tons.

Were these platforms, of such unearthly proportions, actually ramps erected by space travelers as launching areas for their trips home?

Mars seen from the largest of its two satellites, Phobos (ten miles in diameter). Mars is the easiest planet in the solar system to observe. It has neither seas nor lakes nor rivers. Mars, like Earth, has four seasons, and it seems possible that its atmosphere contains water vapor. Scientists believe that some minute forms of animal and vegetable life exist on Mars: bacteria, for example, and even forms of mosses and lichens. To be able to fly in such a rarefied atmosphere, a bird would need a wingspan of 50 feet!

Jupiter as seen from one of its twelve moons. Jupiter is the largest planet in the solar system and its diameter (89,000 miles) is over eleven times that of the Earth. The temperature at its surface is —220° F. and its atmosphere seems to consist of hydrogen and helium with clouds of ammonia and methane. The red spot discovered on this planet was first observed in 1875 and it has fascinated astronomers ever since. Some think that it may be a tremendous concentration of hot gases thrown up by an underground volcano while others think that it is an iceberg of frozen ammonia and methane. It is 30,000 miles long in one direction and it covers an area roughly that of the Earth's surface.

Jupiter

This planet, named after the father of the gods, is the biggest one of our system. With a diameter of 89,000 miles, its volume is thirteen hundred times that of Earth. It circles at 483 million miles from the sun and takes twelve years to make the trip. There are no seasons on this planet.

A heavy layer of atmosphere, thousands of miles thick, surrounds Jupiter. It is composed mainly of hydrogen and its surface temperature is about -205° F. Within the atmosphere float clouds of frozen ammonia and methane, gases which are so highly poisonous that it seems impossible that any living creature could survive on this planet. Between these clouds there is a bright red spot, more than twice as wide as the earth. Since Jupiter receives very little of the sun's light and is very cold, astronomers are puzzled by what this red spot could be. They think it is probably a volcano exploding far underneath the layer of ice that coats the whole planet.

The red spot also enables us to see that Jupiter rotates extremely quickly, a complete rotation every ten hours. The enormous centrifugal force that this speed creates makes the gases around Jupiter's equator bulge like a tire, but the gravitational force that its huge mass produces is so strong that it keeps the gases from flying away.

Jupiter has twelve satellites. Four of these twelve moons that circle around it were discovered in 1610 by Galileo, with the help of the telescope he had just constructed. Two are the size of Mercury and the other two are approximately the size of our moon. They whiz around Jupiter at a great speed, the fastest taking two days to circle the planet and the slowest seventeen days. In addition, the building of better telescopes brought about the discovery of eight other tiny moons around Jupiter. Most of these are only a hundred miles in diameter and are probably made of rock. Some may even be ice or condensed ammonia gas. The latest satellite to be discovered was spotted for the first time in 1953. All four of the moons seen by Galileo rotate at the same speed as they travel around the planet. Thus they always keep the same face pointing toward Jupiter, just as our own moon does to its planet.

We have received radio signals from the planet Jupiter. These static-like sounds are thought to be the result of thunderstorms in its tremendously thick and unusual atmosphere.

The first practical measurements of the speed of light were made by the Danish astronomer Ole Roemer as early as 1675, while he was observing the movement of some of Jupiter's moons.

Saturn

Saturn is the golden planet. In the night sky it looks like the brightest yellow star, although when looking at it closely, we see that, like all planets, it twinkles less. Although it is the sixth planet away from the sun, it shines so brightly because it is big—almost as big as Jupiter. Its diameter is 71,500 miles and its gravitational pull is almost as strong as Jupiter's. Like Jupiter, it makes a complete rotation every ten hours, but its year, the time it takes to complete its orbit around the sun, is the equivalent of 29 1/2 of our years. Because it is so far away from the sun, it, too, must be very cold.

Saturn's volume is eight hundred times as great as Earth's, but its mass is one hundred times lighter. If instead of whirling in space Saturn floated on an immense ocean, this planet would bob on the surface like a huge rubber ball.

Two lovely rings surround Saturn without touching it. They circle outside of the atmosphere around the equator. Because they are only ten miles thick they are transparent. The closest one is seven thousand miles from the planet and is very thin. (Neither can be seen without a telescope.) A black band separates it from the next one which is wide and bright. The combined width of the rings and the distance between them is forty thousand miles.

The inner ring turns completely in seven hours, hence faster than Saturn itself. Saturn appears to be the only heavenly body with rings, and the rings themselves are puzzling. Perhaps they are crystals of ice, or dust particles from moons which have long ago broken up.

Ten moons circle Saturn. The biggest, Titan, is the size of our moon. Nine of the moons turn in the same direction as their planet. The farthest out, Phœbe, turns in the opposite direction.

Saturn as seen from one of its ten satellites. This planet's double ring consists of millions of fragments of different sizes, the residue of one or more satellites which exploded several million years ago. The surface of the planet may be one huge ocean of liquid hydrogen.

All planets of the solar system travel about the sun in the same direction. Eight rotate on their own axes like the blades of a helicopter, in a clockwise direction. Uranus is the exception to this rule. Its rotation is similar to that of an airplane propeller; it moves in a spiral, counterclockwise direction.

From Neptune's icy surface (— 200° C.) the sun is but a small circle of light. One of Neptune's two satellites remained undiscovered until 1949.

Uranus

In Greek mythology, Uranus is the god of heaven. In the sky, the planet Uranus glows with a strange greenish light.

When the German, William Herschel, came to London to be an organist, he already was more interested in astronomy than in his music. He built in his own workshop telescopes that were the most powerful then known in the world. On the thirteenth of March, 1781, Herschel was observing a group of stars in the Gemini constellation when he noticed that one of them was slightly bigger than the others and glowed with a greenish light. He had just discovered the seventh planet of our solar system, Uranus.

Astronomers then set about studying the movement of this new planet. They found that Uranus is 1,782 million miles away from the sun, that it takes eighty-four of our years to circle the sun and that it rotates on its axis every eleven hours. Though Uranus is four times as big as the earth, the force of gravity on its surface is almost the same as that on our own planet.

Herschel himself discovered the largest two of Uranus' five moons in 1787 and named them Titania and Oberon. Two more moons were first seen in 1851 and the last was not discovered until 1948. All of the moons are very small, and the largest, Titania, is only sixty miles in diameter. The orbits of all Uranus' moons are tilted about 90° from the planet's equator and they appear, in a telescope, to travel in an almost north-south direction.

Neptune

Sixty-five years after Herschel spotted Uranus, Neptune was discovered by mathematical calculations. The slightly irregular orbit of Uranus seemed to violate Newton's law. Two astronomers, Le Verrier in France and Adams in England, calculated that the irregularity of this course must be due to the presence of still another undiscovered planet. Their telescopes were not powerful enough to spot this planet, but Le Verrier calculated its exact location. A few days later, Galle, at the Observatory of Berlin, spotted the new planet, less than one minute off the location which Le Verrier had predicted mathematically. Neptune was added to the solar family.

Invisible to the eye without a telescope, Neptune orbits at 2,793 million miles from the sun. It takes 165 years to make the round. So far away from the sun, it receives one nine-hundredth of the heat and light that we do.

Neptune has two moons: Triton and Nereid, the latter discovered by Kuiper in 1949.

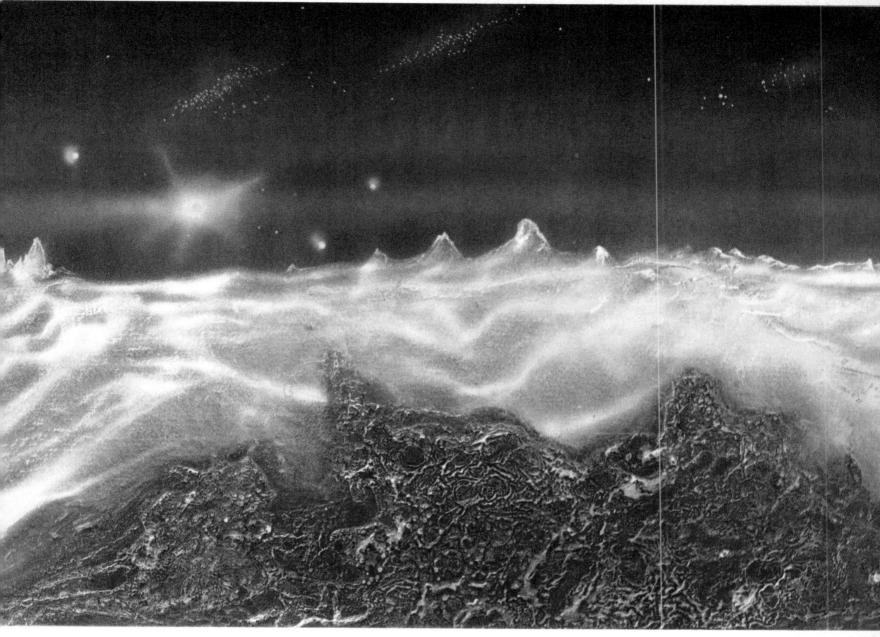

Astronomers think Pluto may once have been a satellite of Neptune, and that it escaped this large planet's gravitational field to take up its own orbit about the sun. Seen from Pluto, the sun is just another star, though slightly brighter than the rest.

Pluto

Irregularities in the course of Neptune made scientists suspect the existence of still another and even more distant planet.

Percival Lowell and W.H. Pickering, two American astronomers, started to investigate. From 1905 onward, Lowell searched the sky for this planet at the new observatory he had established at Flagstaff, in Arizona.

After Lowell's death, other astronomers carried on his researches.

Millions of photographs were taken with a new apparatus which enables two separate photographs of the same sector of the sky, taken at different times, to be compared.

On the twenty-first of January, 1930, C.W. Tom-baugh finally discovered the unknown planet by means of these photographs. It was called Pluto, after the Roman god who reigned over the underworld. The name is appropriate for a planet which orbits in total darkness at an average distance of about 3,670 million miles from the sun.

Though Pluto is not much smaller than Mars, it is so far away and so faint that it can be seen only with a twenty-inch telescope. As a result not much is yet known about the outermost planet of our system, except that its orbit is so eccentric that at times (in 1989, for instance) it will be actually closer to the sun than Neptune. We do not even know if it has any moons.

Are there any more planets besides Pluto in our solar system? Possibly our mathematicians and astronomers will be able to tell us one of these days.

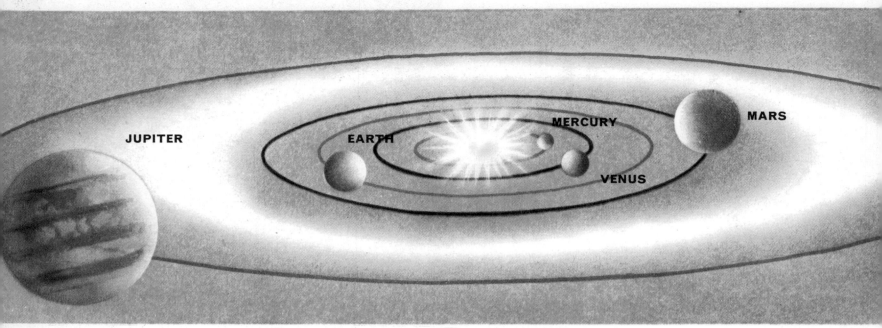

JUPITER

EARTH

MERCURY

MARS

VENUS

One of the great mysteries of the solar system is the presence of thousands of asteroids orbiting around the sun between Mars and Jupiter. In 1805, the German astronomer Olbers thought they might be the remains of a planetary explosion which had occurred a very long time ago, and so the theoretical name of Asteroida or Olbers' Planet is occasionally given this ghost of the solar system. The largest asteroids are considerably smaller than our moon, and their shape is not spherical but irregular. (Eros, for instance, is shaped like a cigar.) They seem to be composed mainly of iron.

◀ The first asteroid to be named was named after Ceres, the Sicilian goddess of agriculture. Piazzi, the Sicilian astronomer who spotted it on January 1, 1801, first thought that he had seen a comet.

The comparative size of the moon and the first four of the larger asteroids, in the order of their discovery. From left to right: **Ceres, Pallas, Juno,** and **Vesta.**

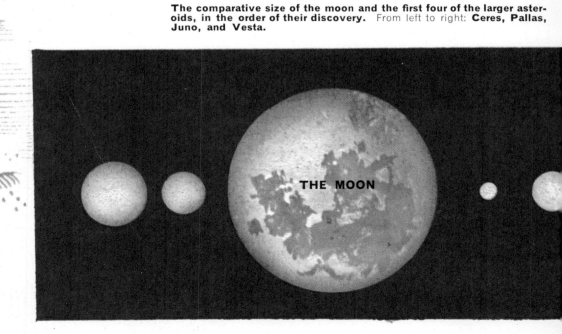

THE MOON

THE ASTEROIDS, METEORS AND COMETS

A space over 350 million miles wide separates Mars and Jupiter. For a long time before they could see them, astronomers believed that there were bodies circling in this part of space. These are, in fact, asteroids, or small planets: dwarf bodies which form a kind of circlet between Jupiter and Mars. Although the number of asteroids is very large, their total mass is less than one hundredth that of Mars.

In 1850, only four asteroids were known: Ceres, Pallas, Vesta, and Juno. The first, Ceres, was discovered by Piazzi in 1801. It is 480 miles wide. Its sister planets are far smaller. Most of them are less than thirty-five miles in diameter. Some, in fact, are the size of large rocks.

A hundred years later there were not enough names of ancient gods, goddesses, and heroes to use for all the asteroids which were known to exist. In 1953 almost sixteen hundred had already been catalogued. Many were given girls' names and a few have been named after states.

What led to the "discovery" and identification of these millions of small bodies was the invention of an apparatus called an *equatorial* which enables stars to be photographed clearly despite the movement of the earth. The equatorial forms part of a telescope. The earth's motion appears to make the whole heavens rotate. The equatorial is pointed at a certain group of stars. A clockwork or electric mechanism causes the instrument to turn at a speed that neutralizes the earth's rotation. Thus the object lens of the telescope remains pointed at the single group of stars. A photographic plate is put under the object lens.

Because the equatorial is set to follow the stars, they appear as solid dots on the photographic plate. The faster-moving asteroids, moving quicker than the camera, appear as lines of light stretching among stars. These lines are recorded and identified.

The 32-inch refracting lens of the Observatory of Meudon in France.

Each asteroid follows a separate orbit and none travel at the same speed.

Sometimes some of these small planets pass very close to the earth. Eros comes as close as fourteen million miles. Apollo and Adonis come even closer. Hermes, whose orbit crosses that of the earth, comes as close as a million miles to the earth.

We do not know how the asteroids originated. One theory is that they are shattered bits from a dead planet.

Because they are in orbits like the planets, none of these huge blocks of matter come sufficiently close to the earth to crash into our planet.

Meteors

On fine nights in April or August we can see small, bright streaks traveling across the sky. People often

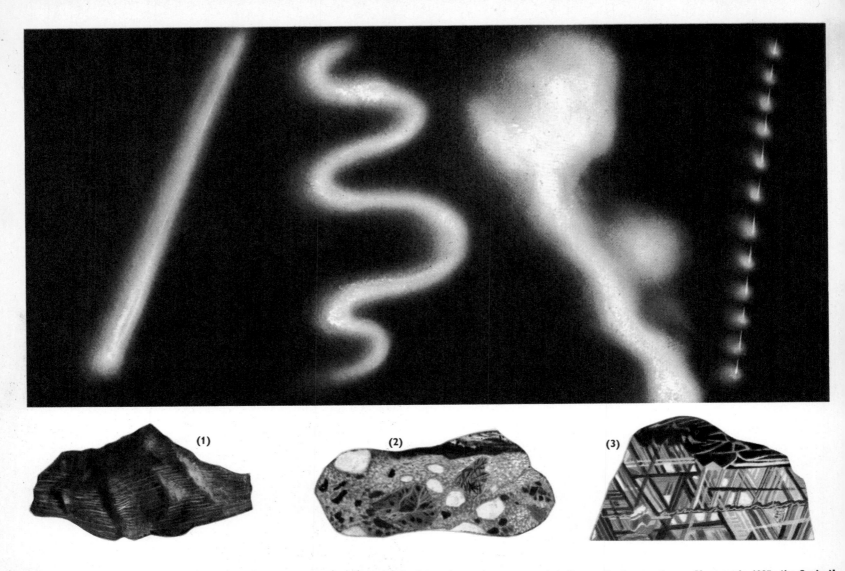

Above, from left to right: **The straight path of a meteor in the upper levels of the atmosphere ; an undulating path observed over Norway in 1935 ; the fireball of a meteor over America in 1933 ; the photographic track (10 photos per second) of a shooting star in the Perseids.** 1. **A 40-pound meteorite which fell in Upper-Volta.** 2. **A stone and iron meteorite weighing 10 pounds which fell in Mauretania.** 3. **The presence of iron in a meteorite can be proved by an acid which attacks iron phosphides and streaks its polished surface.** One of the most amazing chapters in the history of meteorites started with a stone shower in France in 1864 and ended with a fantastic discovery made in America in 1961. Around eight o'clock on the evening of May 14, 1864, all France thought the moon had left its orbit. Actually it was a meteor of extraordinary size. A few minutes later, enormous thunderclaps were heard, and a rain of stones fell on the village of Orgueil in the region of Tarn-et-Garonne. When, in January, 1961, American scientists examined fragments of this shower which had been preserved in New York's Museum of Natural History, they found not only crystalized salts, iron and magnesium carbonates and iron sulfide, but a strange black substance of organic origin. This meant that living matter had been on the meteor!

call them "shooting stars." Actually they are not stars at all but bits of matter from outer space. They are called meteors.

Meteors may have been in orbit or may have been floating in space until they came near to the earth and gravitational attraction caused them to bend in to a collision path with the earth. As they enter the earth's atmosphere, friction created by the speed at which they travel causes them to light up. Sometimes they burn up entirely; sometimes they leave the atmosphere, dim out, and continue on their orbit; and sometimes, attracted by the earth's pull, they fall to earth.

Astronomers estimate that billions of meteors reach the ground each day. Most of them are no bigger than tiny pebbles and some are so small that they cannot be seen. Nevertheless it has been estimated that they add to the earth's weight at the rate of eight or ten tons a day. We are continually growing!

These fragments of meteors that reach the ground are called *meteorites*. They look like rust-covered sponges and are classed in one of three types, depending on their composition. Some are metallic (iron and nickel); others are stone and metal agglomerates; and others are mostly stone. They usually fall singly, but they may appear as a group. In 1803 a rain of meteorites fell on the town of Laigle in France.

Not all meteorites are small, however. Some very big ones have fallen to earth and have provided astronomers with rich specimens to study. A block weighing a million tons once fell in Mauretania.

Another giant meteorite dug the famous Diabolo crater in Arizona. The crater is almost a mile wide. The meteorite must have exploded after landing for no traces of it remain. However, we can tell by the age of the trees that grow at the crater's edges that it landed a relatively long time ago, far longer than the one which devastated a region thirty-five miles wide in Siberia in June, 1908. Fifteen hundred reindeer were killed as a result of that meteorite, and the noise from the explosion was heard for four hundred miles.

Actually the percentage of meteors that reach the ground is very small. Since they are usually tiny, and since they begin to glow fifty to seventy-five miles up, most of them burn up before they reach the ground. They burn in varying colors, but most are yellow, white, or blue. Fireballs or bolides are the names we give to the brighter ones. The streak they form is thicker and their path is crooked. Sometimes we see them exploding several times in their course, lovely fireworks in a spring or autumn sky.

It has been observed that a shower of meteors is often seen in the sky after the passage of a comet. Astronomers have deduced from this that a comet's head is composed of meteors traveling very closely together and that comets are fragile and disintegrate easily. Meteors are also often slow travelers. A comet will pass through our orbit and leave a shower of meteors behind it which will continue in our orbit until they come in contact with the earth's atmosphere and begin to burn.

Other meteors have stayed in their orbit for many years and come back each year like stars or asteroids do. About the tenth of August the Perseids swarm, named after Perseus, appears. They were so named because they appeared in the earth's atmosphere in the direction of Perseus. The Leonids cross the sky during the nights of the fourth to the eighth of November. Thirteen days later the Andromeda swarm appears.

When we think that a billion meteors reach Earth each day, it is difficult even to imagine the huge number of them that must be floating throughout all of space.

Meteor Crater in Arizona is the largest and most famous crater caused by meteorites on our planet. Electromagnetic soundings have shown that a considerable mass of iron is buried about 650 feet below its surface. Calculations have shown that the exposed land-mass of the Earth receives but one giant meteorite every million years, yet a Royal Canadian Air Force photographic survey has revealed over ten meteorite craters measuring more than 1,000 yards in diameter on Canadian territory alone.

Comets

Comets are unusual travelers in our solar system. They visit us and spread their magnificent tails across the starry heavens. We do not know very much about them.

The head of a comet consists of a nucleus which is surrounded by a luminous, thin cloud. The nucleus, as we have said, is probably made up of meteor fragments held closely together. Comets are not self-luminous but reflect the light of the sun.

In its wake the comet drags a luminous tail of rarefied gas which is so light and transparent that we can see the stars through it. The earth has passed through the tail of Halley's comet with no ill effect. The tail of a comet may be many millions of miles long, and sometimes a comet will have more than one. The Chéseaux comet of 1774 had six tails which were clearly visible by daylight.

The tail always extends away from the sun, which seems to repel it because of radiation pressure.

Comets follow huge curved paths, many of which are ellipses, as are the paths of the planets. In these cases they return at regular intervals. Halley's comet returns within our view every seventy-five years. Because of a comet's flimsiness there is no strong central gravitational force to hold it together, as a planet is held. Sometimes it disintegrates when different parts of it encounter different gravitational and radiation pressure forces.

Since ancient times men have been superstitious about comets and have felt that their appearance foretold disasters. They have been blamed for extraordinary things.

The 1811 comet had a tail 90 million miles long. French wine growers believed that it was the reason for the exceptional quality of the wine that year.

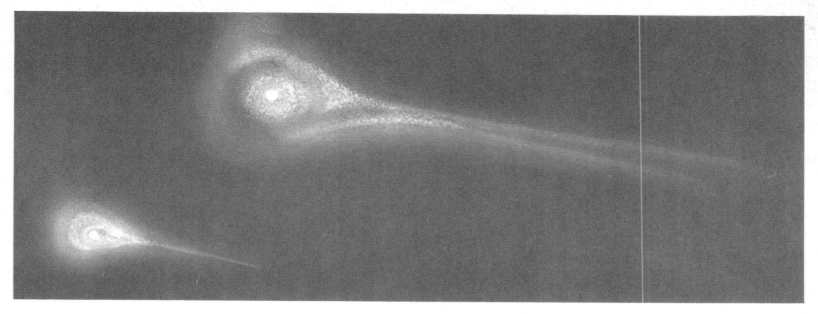

The Biela double comet. Astronomers are still uncertain as to why comets glow and as to the origin and composition of their nuclei. It is quite possible that they are made up of ice crystals, ammonia, methane, carbon dioxide, and hydrogen compounds, and it is also quite possible that frozen gases came from a planet that exploded between Mars and Jupiter some 50 million years ago.

◄ From left to right: **Halley's comet, Donatti's comet,** and **Morehouse's comet.** Mankind has been able to observe thirty-two passages of Halley's comet since it was recorded for the first time in 467 B.C.

The same comet was blamed, however, for Napoleon's defeat in Russia and for the American War of 1812.

The Biela comet, discovered in 1826, enabled astronomers to witness an interesting celestial phenomenon. This periodic comet reappeared at a little over six-year intervals. In 1846, it split in two and astronomers saw both parts of the comet disappear into the distance. Its reappearance in 1852 was eagerly awaited. Both parts reappeared, now considerably wider apart but still traveling together. But in 1859 astronomers looked in vain for the comet.

What had happened to it? They found out on the twenty-seventh of November, 1872. A brilliant swarm of "shooting stars" crossed the sky on the very day on which it was calculated that the comet should have passed. The same procession of asteroids reappeared thirteen years later, in 1886. The comet must have disintegrated into fragments.

Comets follow two different types of trajectories. One is a closed curve and resembles the elliptical orbits of the planets, while the other is an open curve whose arcs become more and more separated. The first means that the planet is a wandering member of its own solar system; the second indicates that the planet is escaping the sun's gravitational pull.

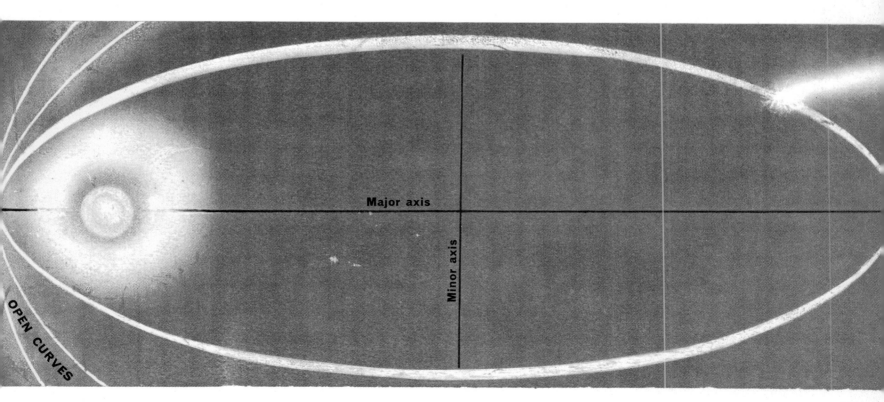

OPEN CURVES

Major axis

Minor axis

THE FRONTIERS OF ASTRONOMY

WITH the help of many kinds of apparatus, astronomers are able to reach out into space. They have discovered solid, gaseous, and luminous masses in the visible universe; and in the part that is still invisible to them they have detected galaxies that they can hear by means of radio. Astrophysicists by their discoveries have been able to demonstrate the extreme minuteness of mankind in comparison to the almost unbelievable size of the universe. Our solar system is but a small cloud of dust lost in the Milky Way. The latter is only a thin, gold-studded circlet in the vast treasure chest of the universe.

At the extreme limits of the heavens there are galaxies consisting of nebulae, star masses, and certainly other solar systems similar to our own. These galaxies appear to form groups in specific sectors of the heavens, particularly in the Virgo constellation. From photographs we have obtained a certain amount of information on their structure. Their most common appearance is in the form of a bright ring around which one or more milky-white spirals appear to revolve. The shining swarm seen through Andromeda is the most famous of these giant space archipelagoes. This constellation of the Northern Hemisphere is 1 1/2 million light-years from the earth.

It is only in fine astrophysical calculations that we dare venture into the vast, silent spaces of the universe. These calculations are so complex that only a handful of specially gifted individuals are able to understand them. The most advanced calculations become inexact as they reach into infinite space; astrophysicists estimate that the universe is spherical in shape with possibly a diameter of ten thousand million light-years.

Before space travel was contemplated, only the most advanced mathematicians had "ventured" into space. Today, astronomers, scientists, engineers, and ordinary citizens follow the course of the first space travelers.

Space travel or interplanetary navigation is but a process of "on the spot" investigation and could never replace telescopes. In fact, the enormous but definite distance that separates the earth from the nearest star provides a barrier that space travelers may never surmount. The age of atomic industry is as yet only in its infancy, and even if man possessed nuclear-powered spaceships, he would have to be satisfied with exploring the planets closest to the earth.

Space travel is, nevertheless, a magnificent scientific adventure that will push back the frontiers of astronomy and will enable observatories to be set up on other planets.

An insight into the progress of astronomy can be made by comparing Galileo's first telescope (1609) with the Yerkes telescope in America (built in 1897 and still the world's largest refractor). The first enlarged a celestial body only three times, while the latter enlarges it about 1,000 times. During the twentieth century, the remarkable development of astrophysics led to a race between refracting and reflecting telescopes as to which could attain the greatest aperture. Reflectors finally won the race (200 inches for the Mount Palomar reflector as against 40 inches for the Yerkes refractor). As the optical qualities of a lens depend upon both its curvature and the uniform consistency of the glass employed, possible defects in a refracting lens increase with its diameter or aperture. The only way to compensate for such defects is to increase the length of the instrument (about 65 feet for a 30-inch aperture). The practical limit of size is about a 40-inch lens. The practical limits of a reflector are considerably larger.

The oldest Eskimo legends say that the first inhabitants of the Far North tried to conquer the sky by riding on the backs of giant falcons.

HOW OLD IS SPACE TRAVEL ?

THE term "space travel" first sprang from the imagination of the French novelist, Rosny the Elder, but the spirit of adventure and the wish to escape are as old as the human race.

Possibly the origin of travel outside the world dates back to legends which held that man had originally come from some other planet. The inhabitants of Oceania, in the central and south Pacific, describe red-headed gods who built mushrooms of baked soil and set them on a course through the stars by shooting them into the heavens! Did these "mushrooms" of an unknown material carry a small monkey, a trained dog, or even those red-headed gods? Legend fails to tell us, but it does suggest that a superior race mysteriously disappeared into the air thousands of years ago. Were those marvelous engineers members of a raiding party from some other planet who left again after having carried out their mission, or were they an extremely clever earthly civilization of which there is now no trace?

Men, particularly poets and writers, have always dreamed of getting to the moon. Using all the knowledge they possessed in their times, they imagined and wrote of fantastic trips through space, some to the moon and some to the planets.

About 400 B.C., Archytas, a scientist and friend of Plato, described an imaginary space flight made on the back of an enormous pigeon.

At that time birds were the sole explorers of the heavens, and men thought that flying was a mysterious power given only to the birds.

In 160 B.C., a Greek writer, Lucian, wrote the first account we have of a voyage to the moon, but he had trouble imagining how his heroes were to get there. Finally he decided that, during a storm, a huge wave—the largest ever seen—had picked up the boat on which they were traveling and hurled it to the moon. The most inspired of later guesses was that of Cyrano de Bergerac, a French writer of the seventeenth century, who spoke of sailing into the starry

African witch-doctors, known as the griots, tell of a tribe in the Congo who tried many, many years ago to climb to heaven on a bamboo tower. ▶ This tale recalls the Bible story of the sons of Noah who built the Tower of Babel for the same purpose.

Tradition in Polynesia claims that a superior race of beings, of mysterious origin, disappeared into the sky millions of years ago.

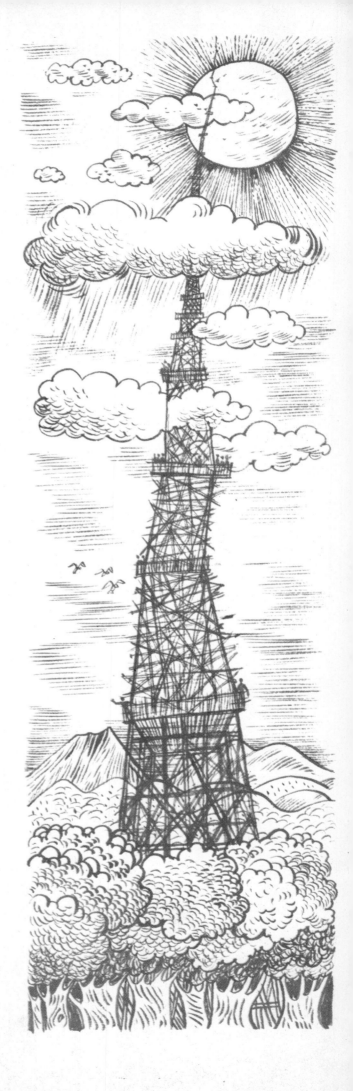

heavens mounted on a grasshopper driven by a "series of saltpetre fireworks." Carbon and saltpetre are the components of black powder. The expression, "a series of saltpetre fireworks," reminds one of rockets that fire in rotation; we could almost say that Cyrano foretold the principle of multi-stage rockets.

About two centuries later, Jules Verne, in two of his novels, *From the Earth to the Moon* and *All Around the Moon*, imagined the travelers launched in a shell. Despite the fantastic dimensions of the cannon he described, the projectile, as he imagined it, would have fallen back to Earth a few minutes after launching.

If men's imaginations first gave birth to the idea of space travel, airplanes, balloons, and hundreds of engineering inventions paved the way to making it possible. The first "space engineers" were poets, writers, and artists; actually, we have to wait until modern times before we can note three famous scientists who will forever mark an important stage in this science. They are Robert Esnault-Peltrie, the first French space pioneer; Wernher von Braun, the inventor of the V-2; and Tziolkowsky, the Russian scientist, who has for thirty years devoted his studies to interplanetary rockets.

The space travel era begins with the rocket era.

In The Story of Dominic Gonzales, written by Francis Godwin in 1638, the hero tames swans and geese and attaches ten of these birds to a kite-like frame by means of ropes and cork collars. After an eleven-day flight, this amazing team finally lands on the moon.

Here is a shell for a moon cannon as imagined by Jules Verne. It was to be used as a means of transportation for the heroes of his books, "From the Earth to the Moon" and "All Around the Moon."

On the extreme right: The most exciting balloon ascension was perhaps that by the French flyer Audouin Dolfuss, in 1959. He rose to a height of 42,500 feet in a magnesium and aluminum nacelle suspended from 104 balloons.

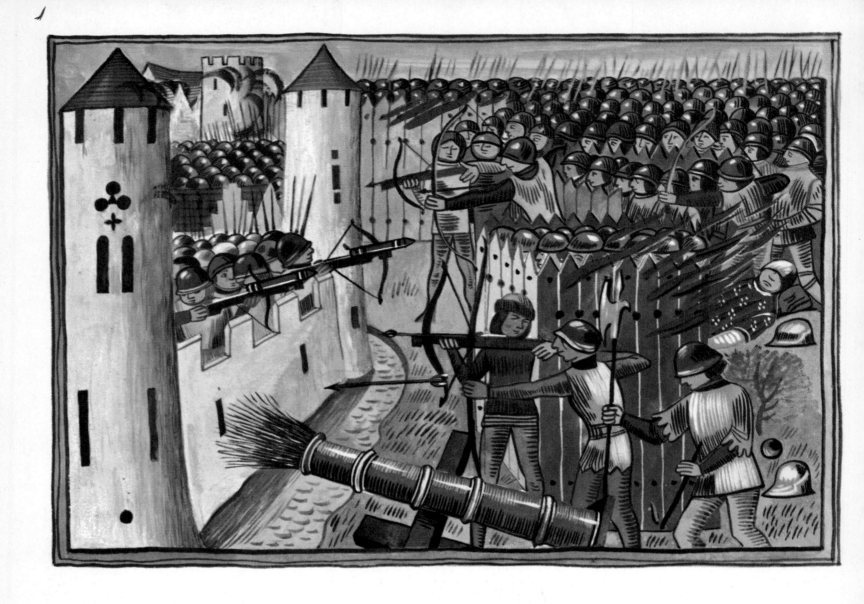

HISTORY OF THE ROCKET

T HE Chinese, after their discovery of gunpowder, were the first to build rockets. Fitted with a bamboo tail, these early projectiles were used as fireworks in religious celebrations. Later, the Chinese conceived the idea of a powder propellant to give greater range to the arrows they shot from their bows. The rockets were fixed to the arrows. The archer set fire to the rocket just before launching the arrow. Soon after it had left the bow the tiny rocket ignited on its course, and the distance the arrow traveled was considerably increased.

This type of rocket-arrow was used in Europe during the Middle Ages.

The real forefather of the electrically fired rockets that were used in the Second World War was the American scientist Robert Goddard of New Orleans. In 1923 he launched the first liquid-fuel rocket.

The principle of action and reaction. From the force of the gas coming from the cartridge, the shell is fired forward and the cannon moves backward. The force of the exploding powder is equal in both directions. The cannon, being heavy, moves slowly and only a few inches, while the lighter shell travels a great distance at high speed. In the same way, the impulse which drives a rocket forward is equal and opposite to the impulse of the gases moving backward. A shell's greatest speed is attained when it leaves the cannon's mouth (initial velocity), but as a rocket is self-propelled, its acceleration only begins when it is fired.

As early as 970 A.D. the Chinese Emperor Tai-Tsu's engineers fixed rockets to their arrows to increase their range. The first incendiary rockets made their appearance in the West during the fifteenth century. During the seige of Orleans (1428), the defending French cross-bowmen used them against British palisades and catapults.

The great Italian painter Leonardo da Vinci (1452-1519) was also the most farseeing military engineer of his time. He conceived of a "fire-wheel" propelled by gunpowder rockets. Like a modern offensive grenade, its primary object was to frighten the enemy.

The military use of rockets spread rapidly from East to West during the first half of the nineteenth century. In 1232, Chinese archers put the Mongol cavalry to flight with "arrow rockets." In 1800 the British expeditionary forces in India were sorely tried by cloth-covered rockets with long bamboo tails attached. In 1807, however, the Royal Navy launched 40,000 incendiary rockets against Copenhagen.

Principal types of military rockets during the nineteenth century:
1. Rocket stabilized by an exterior pine stick (1809)
2. Rocket stabilized by a stick screwed into the center of its base (1826)
3. Explosive rocket (1814)
4. Percussion-cap rocket (1840)
5. Grenade rocket (1840)
6. and 7. Shell-rocket and incendiary rocket (1862)
8. The three elements of an 1849 explosive rocket (explosive charge, coupling screw, and driving mechanism stabilized by fins instead of a stick). The propellant for almost all these rockets was composed of charcoal, saltpetre, sulphur and water. The explosive rockets of 1849 were the forerunners of today's modern mortar shells.

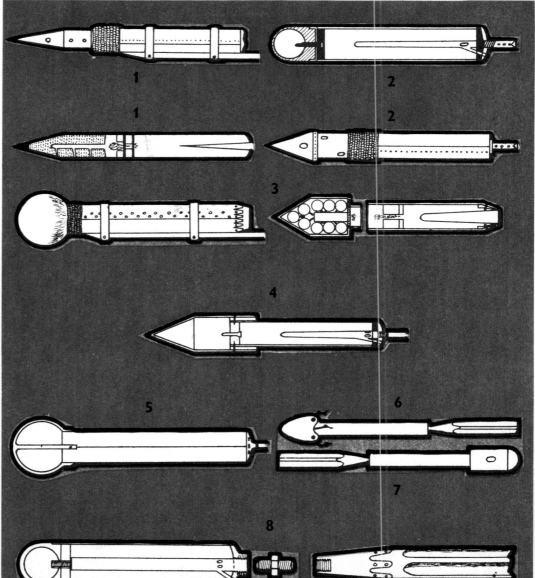

Airborne rockets were first used by the French during the First World War. In 1916, they equipped Nieuport fighters with gunpowder rockets to destroy German observation balloons. The launching rack consisted of a long tube into which the tail stick of the rocket could slide.

Shortly before the end of the Second World War, Wernher von Braun built the V-1's and then the V-2's. The V-1 was a rocket catapulted by a gun and propelled like a shell. The launching was similar to that of the Chinese arrow. During the rocket's course a jet motor came into operation and carried the missile to its target, at four hundred miles per hour.

The V-2's were vaned rockets about fifteen yards in length. They were launched vertically and then at a suitable altitude their course was altered by a gyroscope that controlled their stability. At that date remote control was still unknown, and mathematical calculations entirely controlled the manner of launching.

Principle of the rocket

A rocket is a very simple type of jet propulsion engine. It can be just as well propelled in a void as in the air. It is pushed forward by the gas ejected by the jet nozzle. It is not propelled by pushing against the surrounding air. Pressure operates against the interior of the rocket.

The combustion mixture, usually alcohol and liquid oxygen, explodes in the chamber. The gas issues from the nozzle through a hole in the rear.

Were there no hole, pressure would be applied equally to the whole interior surface. Only while hot gases are ejected from the rear is there a forward thrust on the rocket.

V-1 rockets were known as "buzz bombs." They were supported by wings, stabilized with a rudder, and propelled by a gas jet after being catapulted along a guiding ramp.

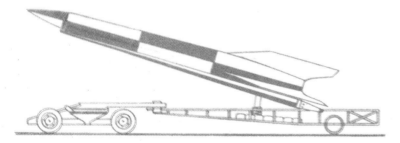

A few facts on the V-2, the radio-controlled flying bomb which paved the way to modern astronautics: Name: Vergeltungswaffe (revenge weapon). First flight: September 6, 1944, at Peenemunde on the Baltic. Nationality: German. Diameter: 67 inches. Weight: 12 1/2 tons, of which 1 ton was explosive. Apogee (highest point of trajectory): 50 miles. Speed: 3,500 miles per hour.

Below: The longitudinal cross-section of a V-2 rocket operating on a mixture of a combustible and a liquid fuel. Such a rocket is powered by combustion gases. The role of the combustive is to ignite and activate the second liquid or fuel. In the sketch below, a tank of compressed air (1) creates pressure in the tanks of combustive (2) and fuel (3). The mixture immediately ignites on reaching the combustion chamber (4). An American, Robert H. Goddard, was the first to design a rocket powered by liquid "propergol" (1926).

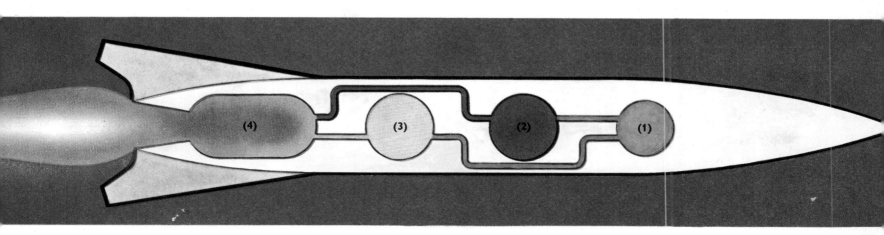

An electric spark sets off the explosion of oxygen and alcohol and the temperature of the explosion chamber immediately rises enormously, to about five thousand degrees. The chamber must therefore be surrounded by a cooling system which keeps the metal walls from melting.

This pushing force, or "kickback," will increase with the quantity of gas expelled and with the speed at which it is expelled. Intercontinental rockets reach a speed of sixteen thousand miles per hour with respect to the earth, while the ejected gas may have a speed of two thousand miles per hour with respect to the rocket.

Multi-stage rockets

The principle of a multi-stage rocket is to add successively to the first stage of the rocket a number of new "pushes." Each stage is almost a rocket by itself and all are fitted within each other. The first has the most power, for its job is to launch the rocket when it is the heaviest. It must both lift the other two rockets and fight the strong pull of the earth's gravi-

tational force. As soon as its combustion fuel is used up, each stage is dropped. A three-stage rocket, consuming as much fuel as a single rocket, would reach a speed almost twice as great.

The American *Far Side*, a three-stage powder rocket, reached a height of four thousand miles after bursting from a plastic balloon that carried it to a height of nineteen miles. To escape from the earth's attraction, an interplanetary rocket must reach a speed of 25,000 miles an hour, or seven miles per second. We call this speed the "speed of escape."

If our Earth were alone in space and if our rocket were not deflected from its course by entering the field of attraction of another planet, it could continue on its course indefinitely.

When the 480-ton Saturn is launched in 1964, it will serve as a testing stand for the giant, 2,000-ton Nova. The Saturn is a three-stage rocket designed to put a 20-ton payload into orbit. Its first stage consists of a group of eight rockets. The Nova super-rocket is aimed at round-trip flights between the Earth and the moon. The astronaut is expected to return to the Earth in a five-ton spaceship.

The main satellite-carrying American rockets : 1. **Juno II** ; 2. **Scout** ; 3. **Thor Able** ; 4. **Thor Agena B** ; 5. **Delta** ; 6. **Atlas** ; 7. **Atlas Able** ; 8. **Atlas Agena B** ; 9. **Centaur** ; 10. **Saturn** ; 11. **Nova**.

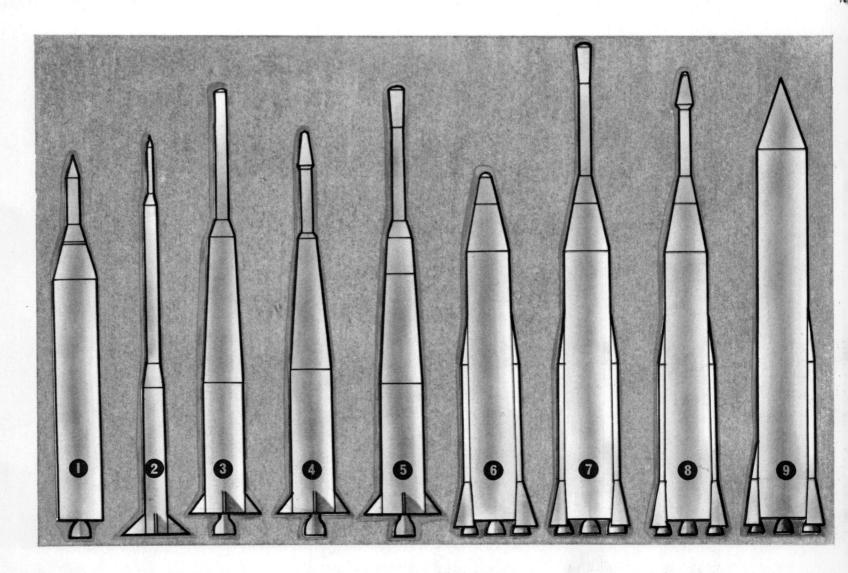

Its speed would, however, gradually decrease as the machine got farther away from the earth. At 6,250 miles its speed would be reduced to 4 1/2 miles per second. The rocket would move farther away indefinitely but more and more slowly. At 625,000 miles its speed would be slightly over half a mile per second.

Let's follow a three-stage rocket in its voyage into space. It will be launched vertically but, unlike our artillery shell, it will rise quite slowly.

Air lines will have been warned. They will have delayed the departure of their aircraft or will have rerouted them.

A team of experts are busy in the launching "shelter" close to the vertical rocket. This shelter is a real push-button workshop. What are all the men up to? A space journey is about to start and the nose of the third stage of the rocket holds the future satellite. Multicolored lights flash and go out. Trembling needles move back and forth across the dials. Recording control apparatus checks that all is in order in the sector that it controls. Stabilization gyroscopes rotate silently. Finally, loudspeakers count down the last seconds before the launching: "Six, five, four, three, two, one, zero...."

At that moment a column of flame bursts from the nozzle with an extremely high whistling sound. Swaying slightly, the rocket rises. Its speed increases rapidly. Twenty seconds later the naked eye can no longer make out the rocket, but only a thin trail of fire that follows it like a comet's tail. In less than three minutes the first stage will have used up its fuel oxidant supply.

The oxidant is used to increase the combustion of the fuel mixture. Oxygen and hydrogen peroxide are oxidants.

On the ground, the men at the controls listen for signals from electronic machines which will tell them that the first stage has fallen away. A few seconds later, they learn that the first stage has dropped, as planned, 250 miles from the launching site.

The propellant of the second stage has taken over its task.

The second stage will carry the rocket to the peak of its flight at about 9,400 miles per hour. Telescopes at various observation bases will then follow the course of the third and last stage, which carries the satellite.

Meanwhile, the temperature of the machine has risen tremendously during its passage through the earth's atmosphere. The cooling system is working at maximum speed. Once the rocket has left the atmosphere, it will jettison its large protective casing which added to its weight.

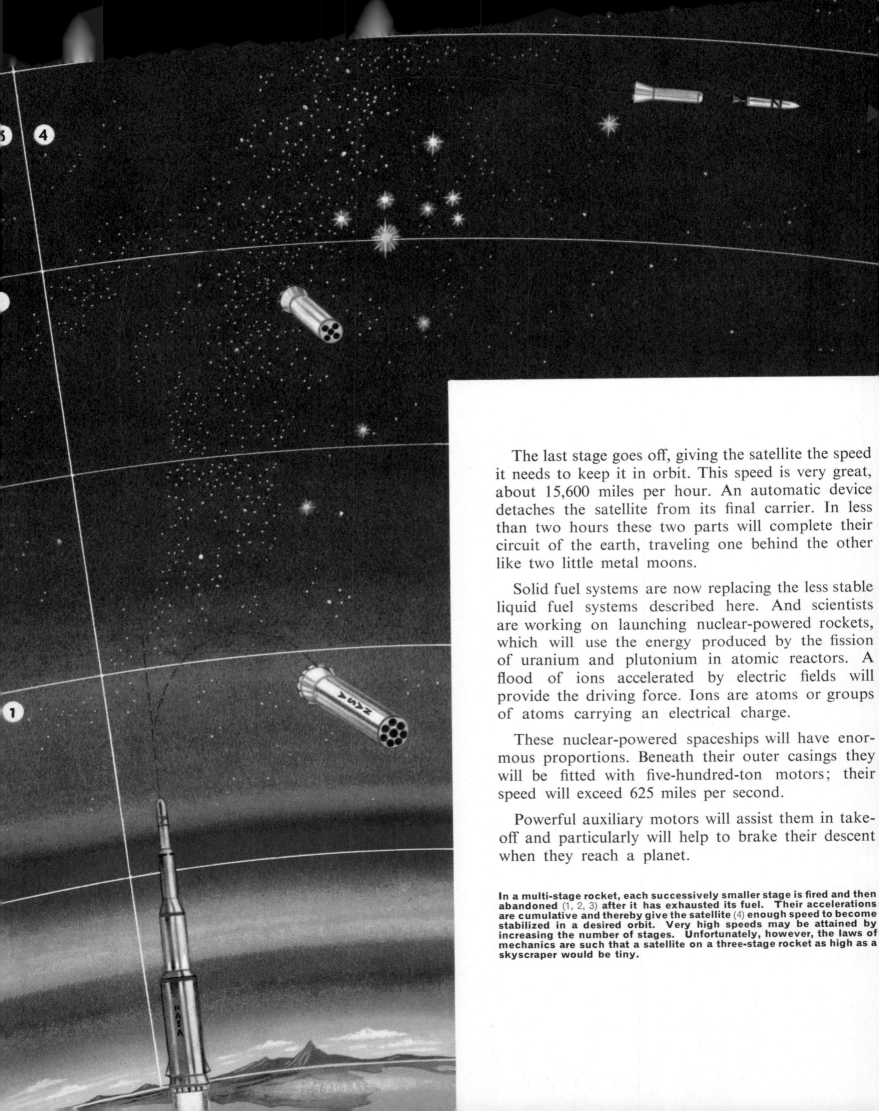

The last stage goes off, giving the satellite the speed it needs to keep it in orbit. This speed is very great, about 15,600 miles per hour. An automatic device detaches the satellite from its final carrier. In less than two hours these two parts will complete their circuit of the earth, traveling one behind the other like two little metal moons.

Solid fuel systems are now replacing the less stable liquid fuel systems described here. And scientists are working on launching nuclear-powered rockets, which will use the energy produced by the fission of uranium and plutonium in atomic reactors. A flood of ions accelerated by electric fields will provide the driving force. Ions are atoms or groups of atoms carrying an electrical charge.

These nuclear-powered spaceships will have enormous proportions. Beneath their outer casings they will be fitted with five-hundred-ton motors; their speed will exceed 625 miles per second.

Powerful auxiliary motors will assist them in take-off and particularly will help to brake their descent when they reach a planet.

In a multi-stage rocket, each successively smaller stage is fired and then abandoned (1, 2, 3) after it has exhausted its fuel. Their accelerations are cumulative and thereby give the satellite (4) enough speed to become stabilized in a desired orbit. Very high speeds may be attained by increasing the number of stages. Unfortunately, however, the laws of mechanics are such that a satellite on a three-stage rocket as high as a skyscraper would be tiny.

The "two hour" observation satellite designed by Wernher von Braun derived its name from the fact that it would orbit the Earth in two hours. The inclination of its orbit to the equator would permit observers to see the entire face of the globe every twenty-four hours.

THE ARTIFICIAL SATELLITE

AN artificial Earth satellite revolves around Earth just as does the moon. An artificial sun satellite is a minute planet launched by man into a much larger orbit. It revolves around the sun. But whatever heavenly body they may orbit, satellites always obey the laws of gravity and of motion. They are attracted by the gravity of Earth or of the sun. The centrifugal force of their orbit prevents them from falling into the body around which they are turning. This centrifugal force balances the force of the body's attraction.

In order to launch an Earth satellite on its trajectory, we have to study the forces involved: the weight of the rocket, the centrifugal force due to Earth's rotation, and the motion of the rocket.

The rocket is launched vertically.

The thrust of the rocket is enormous. It covers the first 7 1/2 miles and atmospheric friction heats it very fast. An automatic controlling device begins to change its inclination. At a height of ninety-four miles the inclination will be about sixty degrees. The first stage then drops off and the second stage goes into operation and will continue to raise the speed of the machine, which now inclines still more.

The third stage adds more velocity to that which has already been built up by the first two stages. The final step is radio-controlled from the ground.

In this the speed of the third stage is carefully adjusted in order that the attraction and the centrifugal force will exactly balance at distance X from the earth. Once this speed has been reached, the power of the third propulsion element is cut. The satellite is in orbit.

A satellite may be shaped like a sphere, a cylinder, or a cone. Jutting out of it are radio antennae that broadcast signals coming in code from radios packed inside. Although these signals are valuable in themselves, it is also very important to recover a satellite once it falls out of its orbit.

The Americans were the first to recover one of their satellites, off Hawaii. In a trip of 470,000 miles, *Discoverer XIII* circled the world for twenty-nine hours before it fell into the Pacific.

One week later, other sensational exploits were successfully carried out by the same technicians. The capsule of *Discoverer XIV* was recovered in flight, and *Echo I*, a U.S. balloon satellite, established the first micro-wave transatlantic radio connection. From Russia, forty-eight hours after the recovery of *Discoverer XIV*, a five-ton cosmic vessel, the *Sputnik V*, after a 43,700-mile space trip, released by remote control a capsule carrying the first space travelers to land safely on the earth; they were the dogs, Strelka and Belka. Successful launchings continue to be reported.

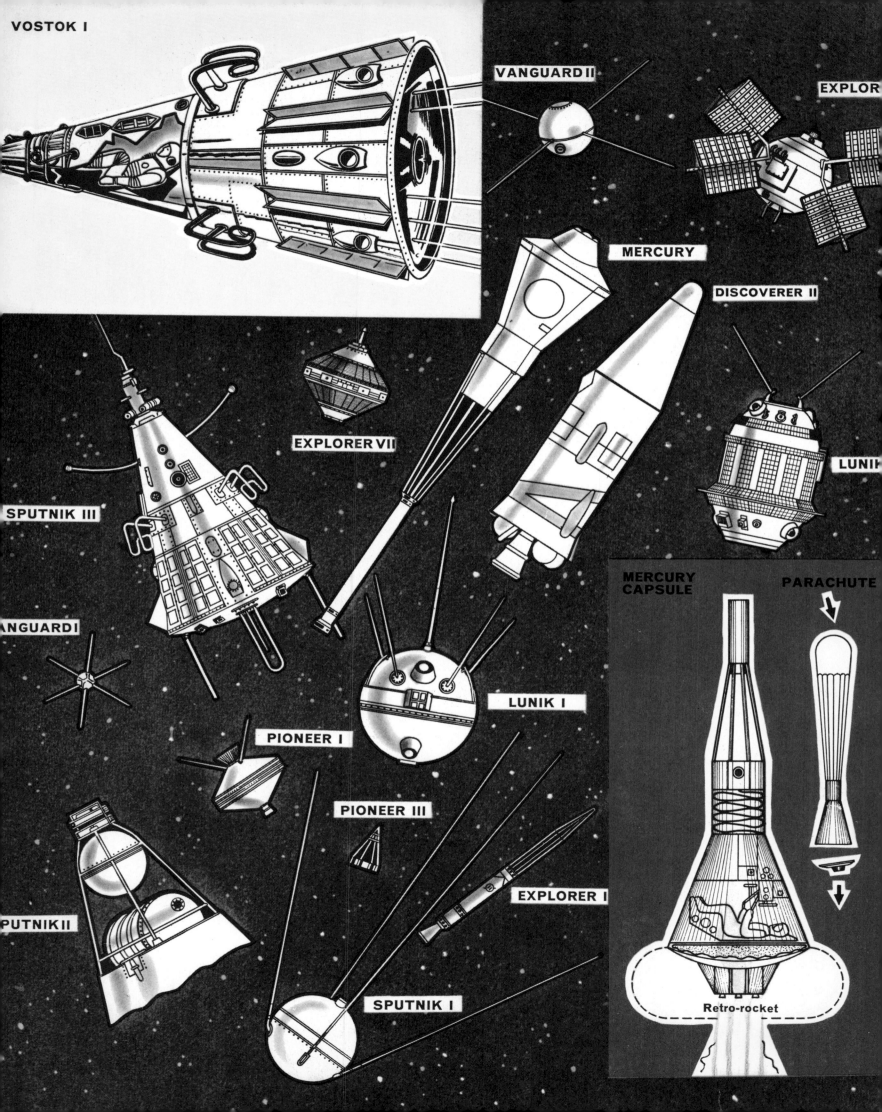

VOSTOK I

VANGUARD II

EXPLOR[ER]

MERCURY

DISCOVERER II

EXPLORER VII

SPUTNIK III

LUNIK

VANGUARD I

LUNIK I

PIONEER I

PIONEER III

EXPLORER I

[S]PUTNIK II

SPUTNIK I

MERCURY CAPSULE

PARACHUTE

Retro-rocket

Explosive bolts separate the satellite from its shell in Discoverer XIII just after it has assumed its downward trajectory.

The little world of the satellites has never stopped expanding since Sputnik I's now famous "beep-beep" was first heard on October 4, 1957. Whatever their mission, each new satellite is a step toward launching men toward the other planets, and little by little each manned capsule is coming closer to being a piloted spaceship capable of making a normal re-entry and landing in the atmosphere. The Mercury capsule will be followed by the Gemini with collapsible wings. Finally, in the Dyna-soar project, the last stage will be a manned rocket-plane.

The different steps in the recovery of Discoverer XIII on August 11, 1960. 1. **When the satellite was over Alaska (seventeenth revolution) it was still in orbit.** 2. **A clockwork mechanism set off rockets which pushed the satellite into a downward trajectory and tilted its heat-resistant nose cone toward the Earth.** 3. **A retro-rocket went into action as soon as the explosive bolts separated the capsule from its shell.** 4. **Gravitational pull increasingly curved the trajectory toward the vertical.** 5. **The breaking parachute opened.** 6. **The capsule floated down near Hawaii. The satellite's position lights and radio beacon enabled the helicopter H to be on the scene.**

American electronics experts have already succeeded in launching a project for a television space relay station. "Telstar," a relay satellite, makes it possible to transmit sound and image signals between the Old and New Worlds. The French were the first to link two continents by television when they sent programs from Paris to Algiers using a relay plane cruising 20,000 feet above the Mediterranean.

To date, the satellites have transmitted to Earth astronomical and meteorological information that we could never have obtained by calculation or from metering instruments at stations on Earth. Satellites can carry cameras, radio transmitters, and television instruments. Traveling in space above Earth, they can improve our meteorological forecasts or can be used for worldwide television coverage. When moving at a great height above Paris to New York, Telstar reflects onto receiving sets in Paris the television waves sent out by American stations.

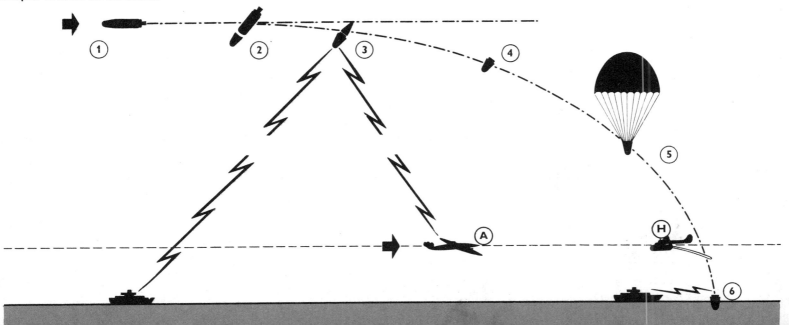

THE INTERPLANETARY STATION

ANY people think that space stations are something invented by science fiction writers and exist only within their books. But different countries have teams of scientists working on plans for very real space stations. Now rocket experts believe that these stations will orbit Earth in great numbers in a few years. Although still on the drawing boards, some very concrete plans have been made for them.

These stations would be enormous artificial satellites. They would orbit Earth in approximately two hours in a zone located at an altitude of between 300 and 625 miles. Initially, they would doubtless be scientific stations equipped with every type of observation instrument and metering appliance used by astronomers, physicists, and meteorologists. Everyone would benefit from them. Astronomers would no longer be hampered by the cloud cover of the earth's atmosphere in their star observations; physi-

cists would study Earth's magnetic field, the ultraviolet rays of the stars, and all the space waves. As for meteorologists, they would be able for the first time to interpret the large-scale movements of cloud systems.

These stations could, at the same time, serve as the first relay stations and future ports of call for the conquerors of space. Cargo spaceships would discharge in their unloading bays prefabricated materials to build stations at greater distances. Communications from *Earth to station* and *station to Earth* would be operated by a regular service of postal rockets which would also carry space technicians. Finally, rockets would be used to move separate prefabricated sections from one spot on the orbit to another.

Let us try to picture this strange workshop. Materials will be received in crates which rockets will launch into the appropriate orbit. Teams of erectors at once start work. Each specialist has been fully trained on Earth to do his task. Unloading the crates of material is a delicate job. The large sections of material float in space as in a stream. There is no weight. Even a gentle push could put a crate out of reach and it would be lost.

Each member of the assembly team has to be very careful in all his movements.

Workers in space are "rocket men." To move about they use small compressed-air rocket motors which are built into their spacesuits. These suits are air-tight, light, and supple diving suits, in which they can work unhampered. Their air supply is provided either by a portable appliance or by a tube from the control cabin. Finally, each man is attached by a long safety line in case his own motor should break down.

These workers can move bulky loads with astonishing ease. The whole team floats around the assembly line without needing scaffolding. Men and materials circle around in the invisible track of the orbit. Engineers and foremen move around in light vehicles to direct the work and to provide the workers' supplies. These miniature spaceships do not need to be aerodynamically designed to move slowly from sector to sector of this circular workshop. They are cylindrical machines powered by two rocket motors, one in front for the reverse and one in the rear for the forward drive. The spaceports will, when completed, look like giant gyroscopes: a huge wheel connected by at least two "spokes" to an enormous hub. Both the spokes and the hub will be hollow and will house mechanical installations and permanent passages to allow the people inside to move about. The interior will be air-conditioned.

Artificial weight will be provided by turning the wheel slowly around its center. This will be necessary because we are all used to walking firmly on the ground and having our tables and chairs stay there, too. The spinning of the wheel will create centrifugal force which will create a false gravity. People inside, able to eat, drink, and work as usual, will find this a great rest from weightlessness.

The station will be protected against the impact of meteorites by a thin but solid casing. Offices, laboratories, observation chambers, dining rooms, dormitories will be fitted out with every modern comfort. Thirty to fifty persons could live in this enclosed space like shipwrecked space travelers on an island 1,250 miles from the earth.

Food supply rockets will deliver the daily needs of this small world, including water, liquid refreshment, and daily oxygen.

If it were found desirable to keep the relay station rotating about the same point, large water tanks could be used to shift the water load to counterbalance the shift of personnel as workers moved about. Automatic mechanisms could be used to move the water ballast as required.

Suppose the third stage of a supply rocket arrives

◀ Upper left: **One of many models of a space station designed by researchers. To be habitable, these enormous satellites must create artificial gravity by rotation, and because of this most of them look like giant tops.**

"Space taxis" will be small rocket-ferries which will operate between freight rockets sent from the Earth and the air-locks of the space stations.

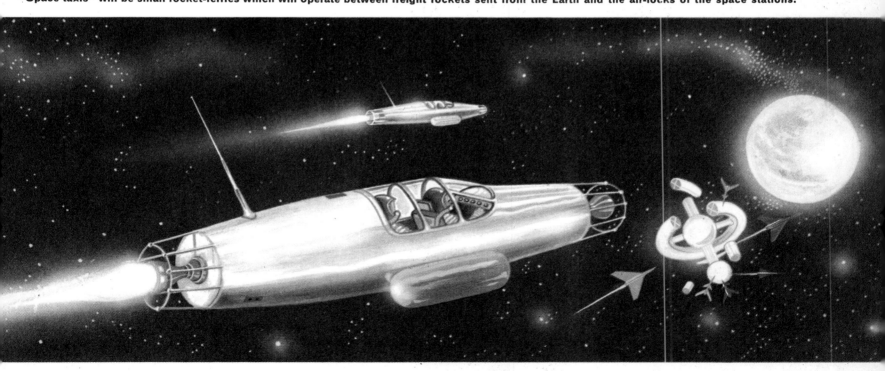

in the station's orbit. It will begin to revolve at the same speed as the satellite. Unloading taxis will shuttle rapidly between the station and the cargo rocket. They will enter and leave the space station by a *lock chamber* in the hub. A lock chamber is a double-doored lock which closes hermetically. This is how it will work when one of the taxis wishes to enter. Immediately the first door opens on the outside. The taxi passes through and stops in a first passageway and the door closes; the second door, leading to the interior of the satellite, now opens and the vehicle enters the station, where it is rapidly unloaded.

The return load of the rocket will be just as heavy as was the load that just arrived. It will include all the rubbish and waste accumulated on board the station. If this were thrown overboard through a porthole it would form a trail of garbage that would follow the interplanetary station indefinitely on its course! It might, however, be possible to get rid of this garbage by launching it toward the earth by means of a small rocket with an easily inflammable casing. The whole load would burn up like a meteorite when it passed through the ionosphere, the upper layer of the earth's atmosphere.

So, in the fantastic world of space stations, perhaps the garbage trucks will be small white rockets and the city dump will be somewhere high in the sky.

◄ Already we can imagine what a building site in space will be like. As there is no weight, workers will be able to move and assemble large sections easily if they themselves are motorized. They will wear pressurized suits and move about by means of small rocket engines powered by hydrogen peroxide or compressed air.

A cosmic tire as imagined by **Wernher von Braun**. Prefabricated sections of plastic and nylon will be inflated and assembled on the spot. When complete it will make a wheel 260 feet in diameter with a hub and two spokes. This tremendous Earth satellite will be an astronomical observatory as well as a fueling station where spaceships may refuel before continuing their interplanetary exploration. ►

1. Landing tube
2. Air-lock for entry or exit
3. Celestial observatory
4. Water recuperation plant
5. Fuel and combustible tanks
6. Air-conditioning plant
7. Electric power plant
8. Attitude control

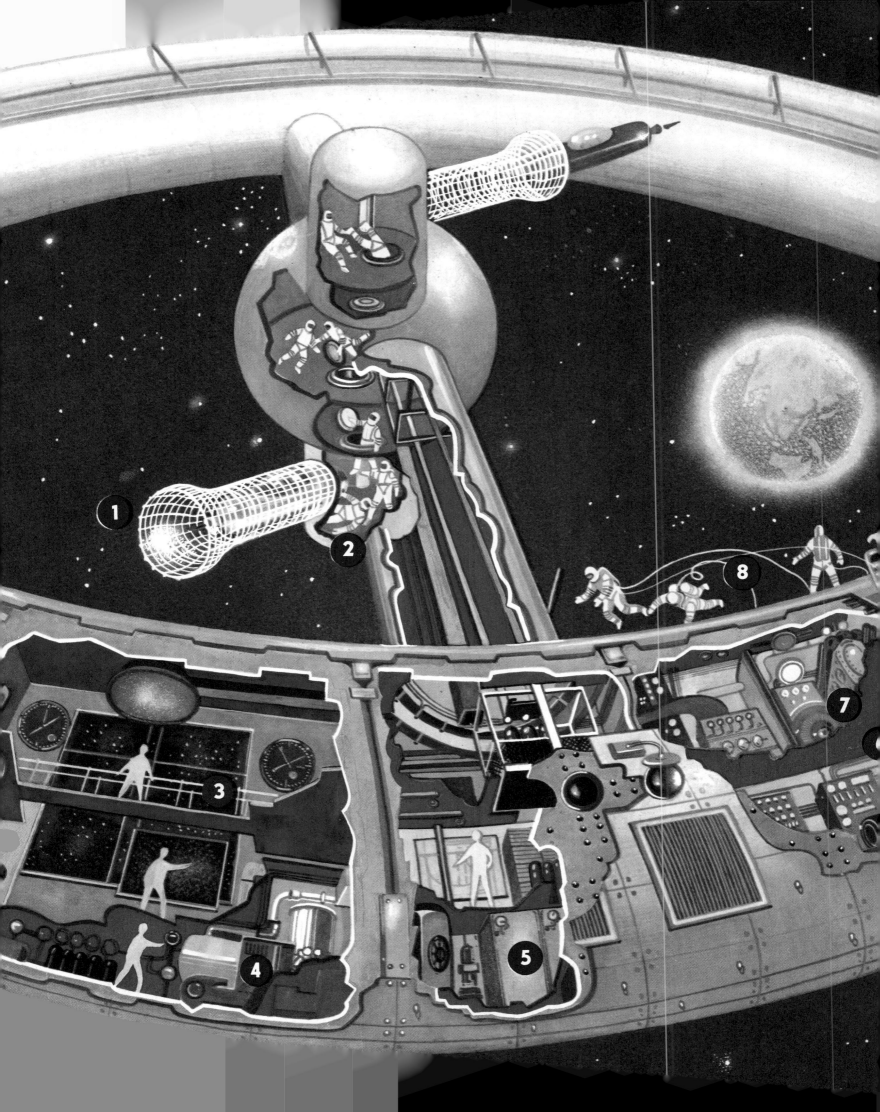

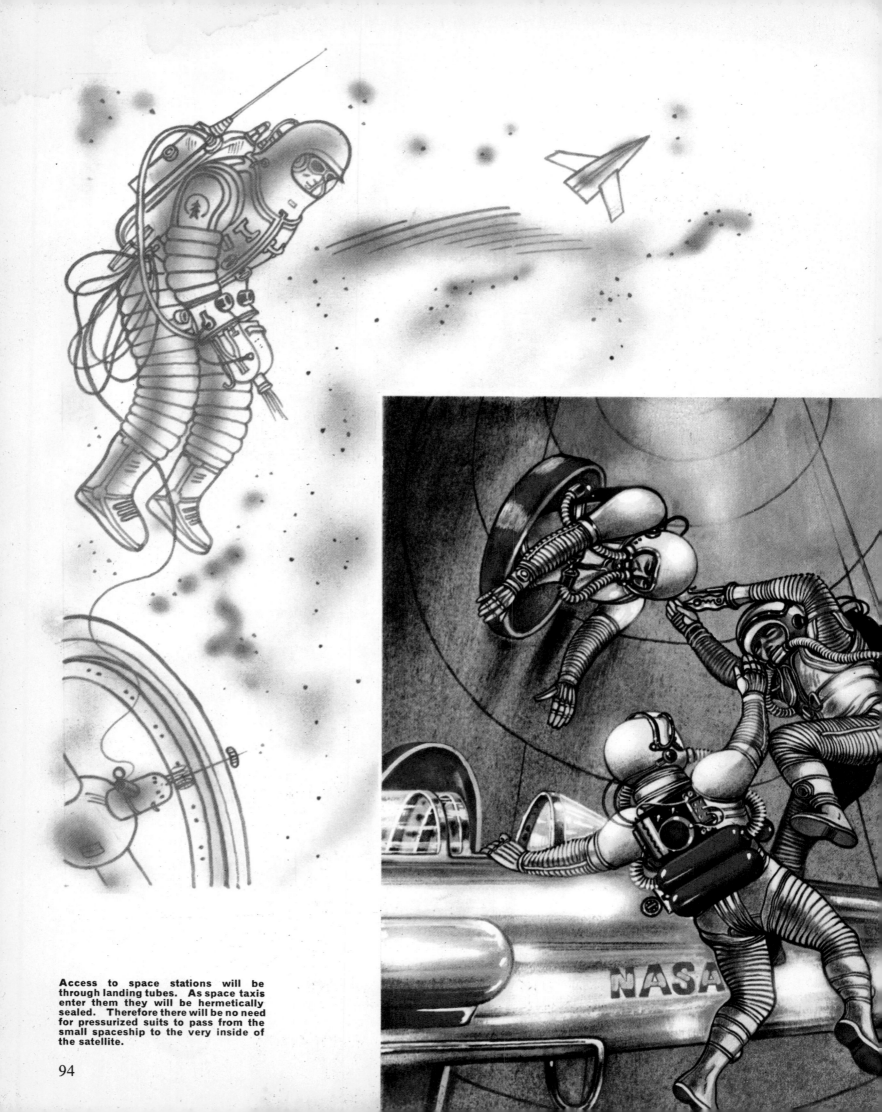

Access to space stations will be through landing tubes. As space taxis enter them they will be hermetically sealed. Therefore there will be no need for pressurized suits to pass from the small spaceship to the very inside of the satellite.

UNDER A FIBER GLASS HELMET...
SPACE PIONEERS

ON the thirty-first of January, 1961, at Cape Canaveral, a Redstone rocket carried Ham into space. Ham was a chimpanzee trained almost as thoroughly as any astronaut. Ham had learned to pull certain levers and push certain buttons. Each time that a little screen in the rocket lighted up blue, Ham knew he was to reach for the blue lever. When he saw the screen was yellow he reached for the yellow lever, and so on.

At Cape Canaveral, observers could follow Ham's trip minute by minute, thanks to instruments in the capsule. They knew that he stayed not only conscious but clearheaded despite the enormous pressure present when the rocket was traveling through the atmosphere, and the weightlessness caused by escape from the earth's gravitational pull. One hundred and fifty miles up, Ham pulled all the right levers on command.

After a flight of thirteen minutes, the capsule came down in the Atlantic, braked by a parachute two yards wide. It was recovered near the Bahama Islands with Ham safe, sound, and calm inside. The flight brought precious information to "Project Mercury": the launching of a man into space.

Two weeks after Ham's firing in America, the Russians put a giant satellite in orbit. It traveled five miles per second. A little while later *Venusik*, an interplanetary missile, was launched from the satellite by remote control. It headed for Venus at a speed of 117,000 kilometers (73,000 miles) per hour. It weighed 14,000 pounds. It took three months to cover the 61 million miles which separate Earth from the mysterious planet.

After preliminary flights in which monkeys and dogs tested physical endurance and *Venusik* tested the use of "space stations," men were ready to try the adventure.

Both the Russians and the Americans picked a group of men and began training them. They were submitted to tests so rigorous they almost seemed superhuman. The astronauts are all magnificent athletes, calm and resolute, sure of themselves and of their physical endurance. They have quick reflexes and great courage.

Astrakan, April 12, 1961 — A few minutes before 9 o'clock in the morning, Yuri Gagarin climbed into the narrow metal cabin of Vostok I and took his place facing a television camera which was to record his slightest move. A knight of the space age, his helmet was a plastic shell, his armor a pressurized suit criss-crossed with tubes and wires, and his charger a spaceship shaped like an artillery shell. In less than two hours, an amazed world knew that he had succeeded in his mission. He had circled the globe in 108 minutes and gone where no man had ever been before— 187 miles above the Earth, traveling at a speed of 24,750 miles per hour!

" I was able to see the Earth," said Gagarin later. " It is covered by a bluish mist. "

Hours were spent by these men in machines that simulated all the conditions of space flight. Not only did the necessary muscles develop, but their bodies grew accustomed to spinning, turning, falling, squeezing, and expanding. Their insides and their lungs were squashed. They were subjected to wind tunnels. They were trained to stay in control of themselves while special machines spun them at tremendous speeds and simulated the effects of acceleration. They fought not to black out.

"G-Day" was the day on which Soviet citizen Yuri Gagarin was launched into space. On April 12, 1961, he rested on a large horizontal couch inside cosmic vessel *Vostok* (East). His head enclosed in a glasslike helmet, his body encased in a pressurized flying suit, he was ready for the final launching. Once more the loudspeaker in the control shelter counted out the final seconds before his departure. It was now 9:07 A.M. The spaceman heard a low rumble; the rocket vibrated; then a tremendous weight stifled and crushed him against his plastic casing.

He was not in sole control. Acceleration was controlled by infinitesimal adjustments that only an automatic pilot could make. The spaceman, however, was immediately able to check that the electronic robot was operating perfectly. He soon noticed a complete absence of weight, but he himself was held in space by straps. He complained, however, that objects in the cabin floated.

Controlled by the electronic robot, the spaceship at first rose vertically through the earth's atmosphere. As soon as it had jettisoned its first stage, the robot slowly but gently inclined the missile's trajectory horizontally. When the second stage ran out of fuel it was also jettisoned by the rocket. The third stage was used to reach the *terminal velocity*, the velocity at which the missile traveled on its chosen course in order to remain on its elliptical trajectory. One and a half minutes after its take-off, the *Vostok* was traveling on this invisible course at a speed of about 25,000 miles per hour.

A camera carried by the missile transmitted a continuous series of pictures of the space traveler. Various instruments recorded his pulse beats and his temperature, for this was the first time that a human body had been subjected to the mechanical forces of outer space. In the complete absence of distracting sound, his heart beats, blood circulation, and breathing sounded extraordinarily loud. Within fifteen minutes Yuri Gagarin was able to observe through the periscope Siberia, Australia, America. The *Vostok* was now traveling in absolute blackness in which the stars no longer twinkled. As dawn broke, the spaceman crossed Africa. A few moments later the remote-controlled robot pilot operated the "return journey" mechanism. The spaceship was moved out of its orbit by decreasing its speed. Braking was effected by starting up retro-rockets operating against the direction of flight of the missile. The spaceship gradually altered its course toward the earth and its atmosphere. The outer casing of the *Vostok* consisted of three separate shells. The first two burned up successively as the spaceship entered the atmosphere. Air friction on the outer surface of the missile acted like a very powerful and protracted application of a brake. By using its two short wide wings, the third shell became a supersonic glider. During the headlong descent the temperature of the third shell was still so high that it became bright red. The temperature in the cabin was tremendous, even though it was insulated from the shell and was refrigerated.

To Gagarin, with his eyes glued to the periscope, the earth appeared to be rushing toward him. Braked by the retro-rockets and by atmospheric friction, the spaceship safely passed through the sound barrier. Soon the reduced speed enabled the robot to be shut off and the final stage of the braking action to be set in motion. Two parachutes were released. A few moments later the launching site came into view and the spaceship, aided by its parachute, landed gently.

Less than a month later, on the fifth of May, Commander Alan Shepard, and his "Mercury" capsule, once more proved that man can conquer space. Launched by a rocket at Cape Canaveral, they performed a 116-mile bound into space, covering a distance of 302 miles. By means of three retro-rockets and two parachutes, the "Mercury" passed through the atmosphere and landed in the sea less than nineteen miles from the point of landing selected. Fifteen minutes after take-off the capsule and its passenger were recovered by helicopter. For the second time, man had managed to free himself from the earth's attraction.

On August 19, 1962, another vital step was taken in man's exploration of space. Russian Major Andrion Nikolaev, the thirty-two-year-old son of a lumberjack, went into orbit aboard Vostok III and was joined twenty-five hours and thirty-two minutes later by Lt. Col. Pavel Popovitch aboard Vostok IV in the same orbit. At times they were less than seventy-five miles apart, and if they had had auxiliary rockets they could have joined. During their joint flight they sang lullabies to each other and ate solid food "as pleasant as in any good restaurant", one of them said later. By the time they had landed within a few minutes of each other near Karaganda in Central Asia on the morning of August 22, Major Nikolaev (or "Falcon," as he called himself over the radio) had completed sixty-four orbits and covered a distance of 1,663,000 miles or three and a half times the round-trip distance to the moon, while Colonel Popovitch ("Golden Eagle") had made forty-eight orbits and covered 1,247,000 miles. They had proved once

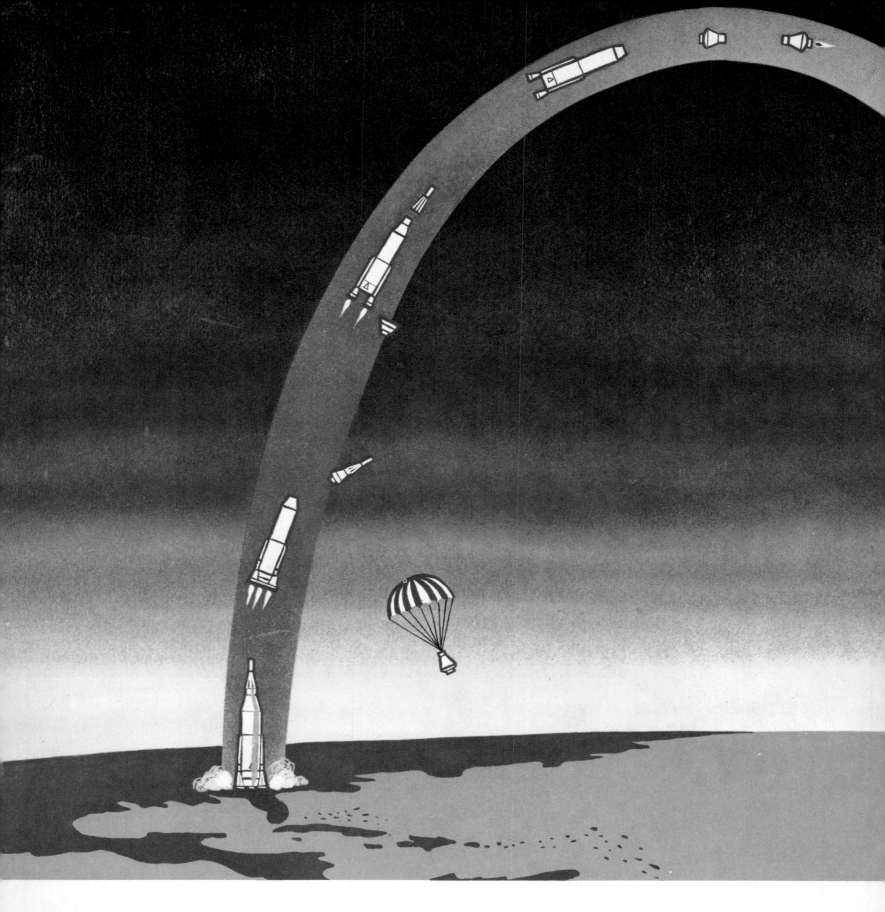

and for all that man can live in space with no ill effects for days at a time.

On May 5 and later on July 21, 1961, the American astronauts Alan Shepard and Virgil Grissom made successful flights in "Mercury" capsules. As we now know, these ballistic flights over the Atlantic Ocean were but tests for Project Mercury's ultimate aim — to put a man in orbit.

The Americans called their first spaceship a capsule because of its shape, a flattened dome in front leading to a truncated cone in the rear (see Mercury capsule, page 84). Landing parachutes are housed in an extension of the cone. The astronaut flies backwards. He is seated while the capsule flies

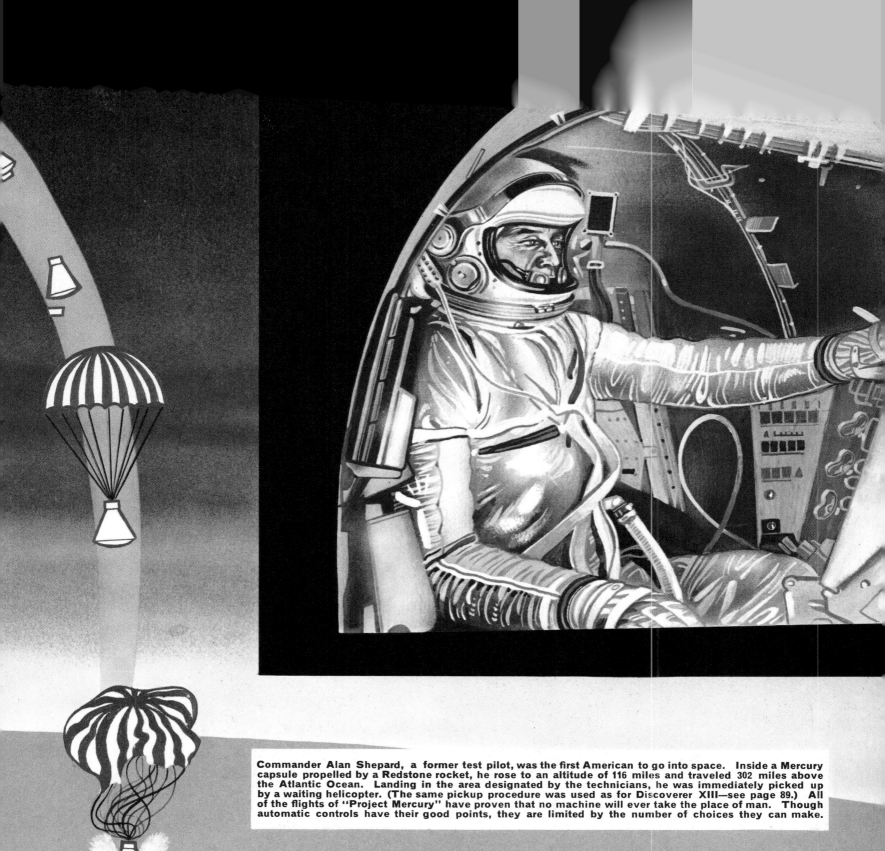

Commander Alan Shepard, a former test pilot, was the first American to go into space. Inside a Mercury capsule propelled by a Redstone rocket, he rose to an altitude of 116 miles and traveled 302 miles above the Atlantic Ocean. Landing in the area designated by the technicians, he was immediately picked up by a waiting helicopter. (The same pickup procedure was used as for Discoverer XIII—see page 89.) All of the flights of "Project Mercury" have proven that no machine will ever take the place of man. Though automatic controls have their good points, they are limited by the number of choices they can make.

about the earth but lying down during take-off and when the capsule tips to re-enter the atmosphere and land. Retro-rockets which slow the capsule down are located in the front, behind the pilot's back, and provide thrust in an opposite direction to the capsule's movement. The parachutes and retro-rockets may be controlled either from the ground or by the pilot himself. The pilot's back is protected by a heat shield consisting of a sheet of beryllium separated from the pilot's seat by a thick mattress of finely ground and compressed nut shells. This combination permits the highly conductive metal to heat rapidly and absorb the sudden rise in temperature due to the friction of air particles against the front of the capsule.

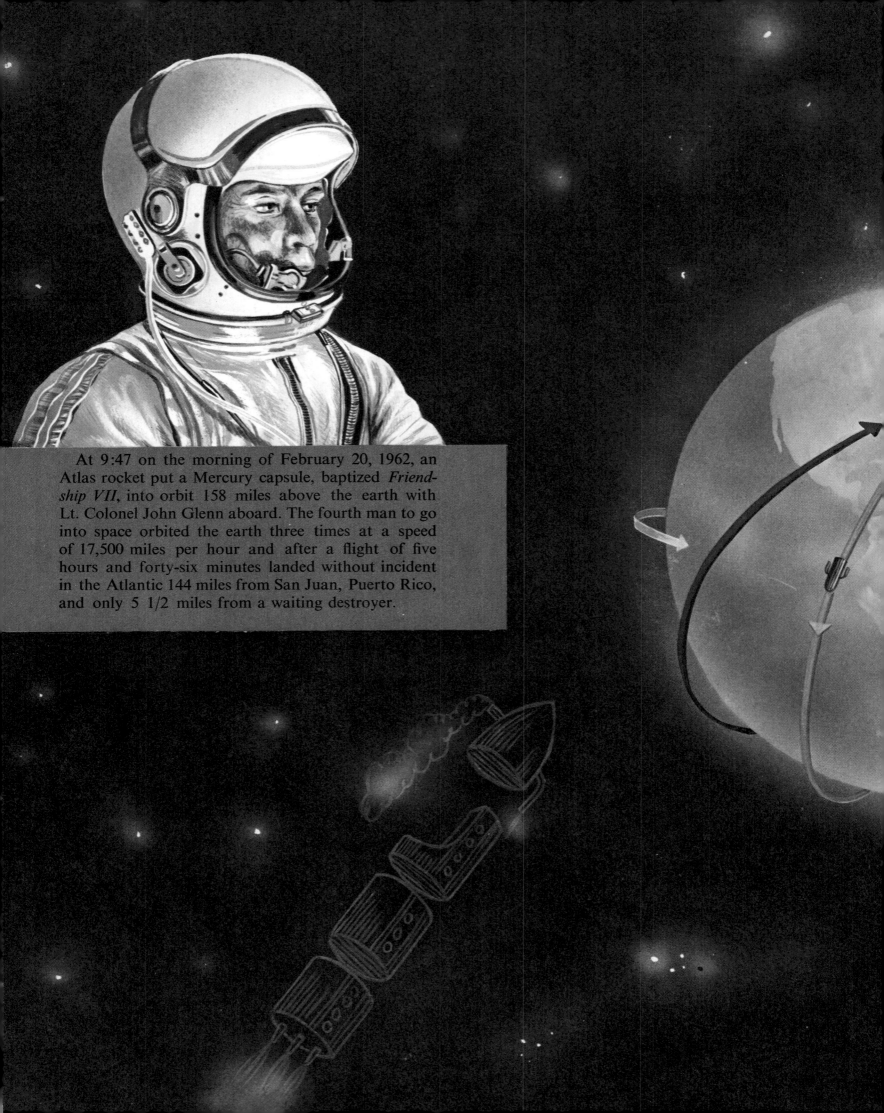

At 9:47 on the morning of February 20, 1962, an Atlas rocket put a Mercury capsule, baptized *Friendship VII*, into orbit 158 miles above the earth with Lt. Colonel John Glenn aboard. The fourth man to go into space orbited the earth three times at a speed of 17,500 miles per hour and after a flight of five hours and forty-six minutes landed without incident in the Atlantic 144 miles from San Juan, Puerto Rico, and only 5 1/2 miles from a waiting destroyer.

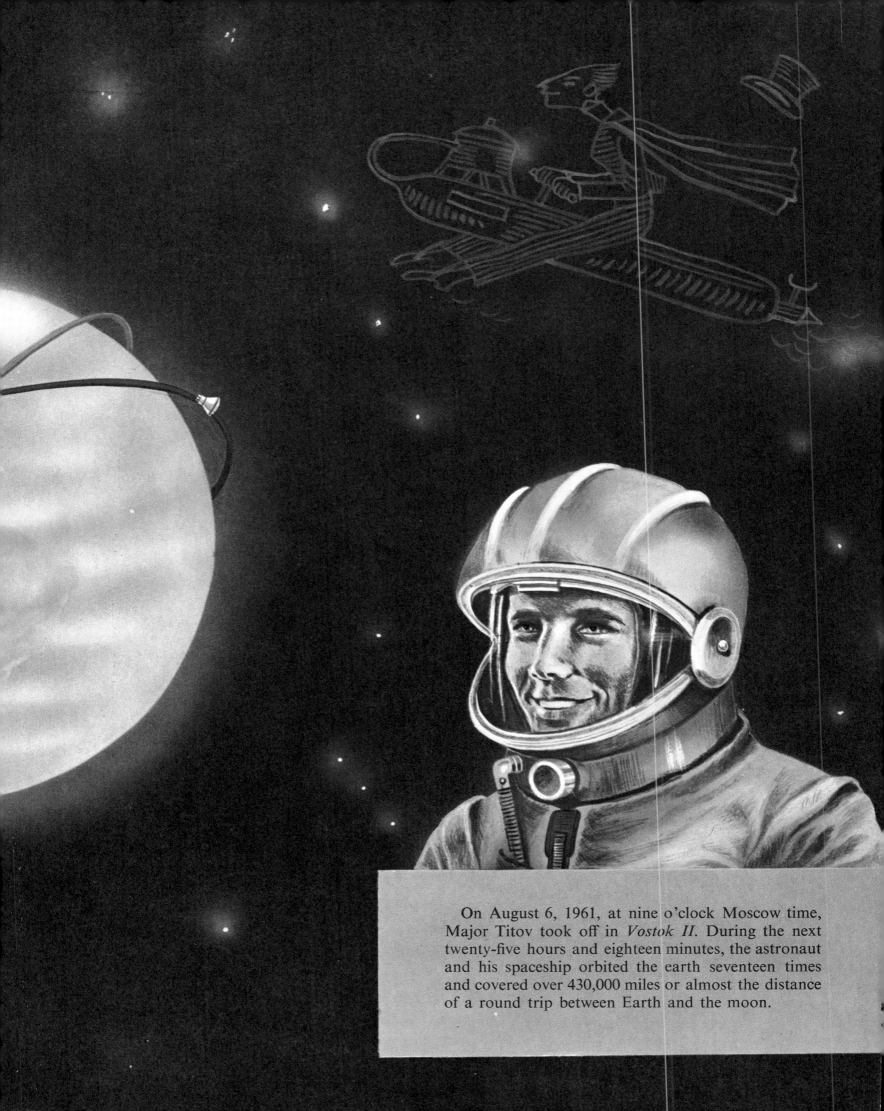

On August 6, 1961, at nine o'clock Moscow time, Major Titov took off in *Vostok II*. During the next twenty-five hours and eighteen minutes, the astronaut and his spaceship orbited the earth seventeen times and covered over 430,000 miles or almost the distance of a round trip between Earth and the moon.

It seems probable that the first men to reach the moon will not leave from the Earth but from a relay-satellite well out of the Earth's atmosphere. As their spaceships will be traveling entirely in space, they will not need to be streamlined like our present rockets which must overcome both the problems of weight and thickness of the atmosphere.

THE COMING CONQUEST

A magnificent prospect awaits mankind. A rocket has already circled our moon. A photographic reconnaissance rocket has photographed and sent back to Earth pictures of the till then unknown surface of the moon.

What shall we be able to do tomorrow? We will make journeys to the planets nearest to the earth; but after that, what? Will men of tomorrow take their vacations on Mars or Venus? Or will men go even farther? A new race of "pioneers" might form: people who know that trips to unknown planetary systems may take more than their lifetime but who will set out with their families anyway.

At the beginning of the century aircraft were creating records of 125 miles per hour. It is not impossible that nuclear spaceships in the year 2000 will travel two hundred times as fast as rockets do today. The new speeds might be in the region of five million miles per hour, or even fourteen thousand miles per second!

One day these super-speed Earth squadrons may set out to solve an enormous problem: whether there are in the universe other planetary systems inhabited by beings like ourselves.

Many scientists today believe that there are. In an attempt to establish contact with other inhabitants of space, American astronomers have tried to pick up radio signals from outer space. Two scientists have studied fragments of a meteorite that fell in California and have discovered that it contained elements that could possibly form the basis of life.

Most astronomers and biologists agree that there are probably over a hundred thousand as yet unseen planets in which life would be possible. Astronomers are almost certain that the stars nearest us serve as suns to planetary systems. Number 61, the Swan, and Number 70, Ophiuchus, might have planets circling around them. Both are less than fifteen light-years away.

What will these inhabitants of other planets look like?

Some scientists believe that three, four, or five thousand million years ago, the human race began with the *Coelacanth* man shaped like a fish. Man has developed to what we all are now, and in the process climatic differences on our own planet have produced such different races as the white, the black, the yellow, and the red races. Intelligent beings of outer space may have taken a thousand and one shapes that we cannot even imagine.

For the present we shall have to confine our researches and hopes to the planets closest to us. Scientists have classified the heavenly bodies of our solar system into three groups. In the first, life would be impossible; these include the moon, Mercury, and Pluto. It would be highly improbable on Jupiter, Uranus, and Neptune. Finally, Mars and Venus may have some vegetation which would make life possible.

All these hypotheses are applicable only if we can suppose that the laws of biology are the same on all planets. Perhaps Martians might classify Earth among the planets on which life as they know it would be impossible.

The first journey to outer space will probably be undertaken by automatic machines. Each reconnaissance rocket will be an observatory and laboratory equipped to carry out a whole series of observations and experiments: the observation of the space through which it travels, the automatic development of long-range photographs, the analysis and microphotography of the atmosphere, and so on. Results will be transmitted to Earth by a radio-television apparatus. Solar energy trapped by mirrors will recharge batteries or operate miniature power plants.

Reconnaissance flights will be followed by actual landings. Here again man will be aided by machines. In America we have constructed a robot excavator. As soon as it touches down, this machine will burrow into the ground, will analyze a sample of the material it digs into, and will transmit its chemical composition by radio.

It is possible that other efficient robots will be used to make preparations for man's first landing, particularly in the artificial establishment of conditions essential to life, such as oxygen-manufacturing workshops and air-conditioned living quarters. These preparations will be followed by numerous experiments in automatic landings. Only after all this will man himself land.

But as always in space, the most important factor will be speed; how to achieve it, how to maintain it, and how to brake it for a landing. We will have to learn to move at speeds we have never before known if we are to plan for landings on other planets.

103

The four or five billion years of man's history are probably only the first stage in his evolution. During the course of this long trail, the extent of man's reasoning and intelligence has developed greatly. It has enabled him to make miraculous progress. What heights has he not already scaled?

Prehistoric man depended entirely on his senses. His sense of smell was almost as important to him as his sense of sight. We no longer use our sense of smell to find meat for lunch. The use we make of our senses is changing. Radar is "seeing" things our eyes could never see; through electronics we hear things our ears couldn't pick up. Speed has allowed us to break the sound barrier. Now man is reaching to a still more daring height, breaking the time barrier.

According to Einstein's theory of relativity, the speed of light is the ultimate speed of the universe. Many scientists have seen the possibility of a spaceship traveling at a speed close to that of light. At this speed a mechanical, physical, and biological breakaway would occur from the time in which the space traveler is living and from the clocks that his spaceship carries. Watches and hearts would beat more slowly. This slowing down would occur all along the line of time, on seconds, minutes, hours, years, to keep pace with the slowing down of the spaceman's own organism.

When he returned to Earth after a two years' journey into space (for the time would be expanded by the speed so nearly that of ultimate speed), the spaceship would be two years older. But our space traveler would no longer recognize his surroundings, since in his absence the earth would have grown one hundred years older!

Light, of course, travels at the same speed from Earth to another planet as from the other planets to us. This, too, will present complications.

Suppose that our Earth spacemen landed on some imaginary planet within a radius of five hundred light-years of the earth. Let us also suppose that this planet is inhabited by beings just like us and that they have television stations just like ours, but considerably more powerful. They would have to wait five hundred years to see on their screens events that are happening here today.

Finally, let us imagine that the dwellers of that mysterious planet possessed telescopes whose range was far greater than anything we have. If they looked through the telescope now they would see three small black objects in the Atlantic Ocean being driven westward by the wind.

These would be Columbus's three ships sailing toward the New World in 1492!

The endsheets: **The angle of the Earth's rotation is such that the sun doesn't set on the North Pole for 189 days of each year. These drawings show the position of the sun on such a day, in the far north of Norway.**

19 h 27
19 hours 27 minutes

20 h 27
20 hours 27 minutes

21 h 27
21 hours 27 minutes

22 h 27
2? hours 27 minutes

23 h 27
?hours 27 mi

0 h 27
our 27 minutes

1 h 27
I hour 27 minutes

2 h 27
2 hours 27 minutes

3 h 27
3 hours 27 minutes

4 h 27
4 hours 27 minutes